PRACTICE
MAKES
PERFECT

Basic
English

Julie Lachance

New York Chicago San Francisco Lisbon London Madrid Mexico City
Milan New Delhi San Juan Seoul Singapore Sydney Toronto

1 2 3 4 5 6 7 8 9 10 11 12 13 14 15 16 17 18 19 20 21   QPD/QPD   0 9 8

ISBN 978-0-07-159762-3
MHID   0-07-159762-X
Library of Congress Control Number: 2007941309

Interior design by Village Typographers, Inc.

McGraw-Hill books are available at special quantity discounts to use as premiums and sales promotions or for use in corporate training programs. To contact a representative, please visit the Contact Us pages at www.mhprofessional.com.

This book is printed on acid-free paper.

*This book is dedicated to my students because they have taught
and given me so much over the years.*

Contents

Introduction

Congratulations on your decision on choosing *Practice Makes Perfect: Basic English* for your first year of English language learning.

There is really only one way to learn a new language, and that is to build your vocabulary, learn the verb tenses and the mechanics of that language, and then practice, practice, practice. This workbook was designed to help you do just that.

This workbook will help you to proficiently learn and effectively master the strategies and methods needed to provide you with a solid foundation in English. All the lessons are presented in a simple and progressive format designed to help you retain the knowledge and gain confidence by applying and reinforcing the skills acquired throughout the workbook.

You will learn the mechanics of English through user-friendly, interactive, and well-constructed grammar exercises. These exercises are loaded with everyday basic words intended to help you quickly and efficiently enrich your vocabulary and give you a firm understanding of the lesson before moving on to the next.

Ample space is provided in each lesson for you to record your new vocabulary words in a central location to allow you to study these words regularly and refer back to them quickly when necessary. Be sure to learn these words by heart as they are basic and useful English words.

Learning a new language is an interesting and exciting journey that is enhanced when the learning material is presented in a stimulating and enjoyable manner that encourages a learner to keep moving forward.

We wish you much success and enjoyment throughout your learning process using this workbook, and we are confident that you will gain from it exactly what was intended: a solid comprehension of your first year of English language learning.

Good luck, and above all, have fun.

To Be: Present Tense

The verb **to be** describes a state of being. Use the following to form the present tense of the verb **to be**.

I am	→	I am happy today.
you are	→	You are smart.
he is	→	He is my friend.
she is	→	She is busy.
it is	→	It is true.
we are	→	We are tired.
they are	→	They are here.

EXERCISE

1·1

Use your dictionary to find the meaning of the new vocabulary words needed for this exercise before you begin. Write the words in your language in the space provided.

_____	flashlight	_____	happy	_____	busy
_____	kitchen	_____	sick	_____	ready
_____	girl	_____	flower	_____	small
_____	vacuum	_____	tent	_____	fridge
_____	counter	_____	toy	_____	floor
_____	basement	_____	ribbon	_____	hair
_____	closet	_____	dirty	_____	tired
_____	today	_____	pink	_____	twins
_____	nice	_____	pretty	_____	true
_____	smart	_____	yellow	_____	friend
_____	here	_____	microwave oven		

*Rewrite the following sentences to create the present tense by choosing the correct form of the verb **to be** in parentheses.*

1. The girl (am, is, are) pretty. _____

2. I (am, is, are) ready. _____

3. She (am, is, are) my friend. _____

4. They (am, is, are) twins. _____

5. The flowers (am, is, are) yellow. _____

6. The flashlight (am, is, are) in the tent. _____

7. The fridge and counter in the kitchen (am, is, are) dirty. _____
   _____

8. I (am, is, are) tired today. _____

9. We (am, is, are) busy. _____

10. The toys (am, is, are) in the basement. _____

11. The ribbons in my hair (am, is, are) pink. _____

12. The kitchen (am, is, are) very small. _____

13. The vacuum (am, is, are) in the closet. _____

14. He (am, is, are) nice. _____

15. The microwave oven (am, is, are) in the kitchen. _____
    _____

16. The toy (am, is, are) on the floor. _____

17. I (am, is, are) sick today. _____

EXERCISE
1·2

Use your dictionary to find the meaning of the new vocabulary words needed for this exercise before you begin. Write the words in your language in the space provided.

_____ aunt	_____ cousin	_____ bald
_____ cloud	_____ uncle	_____ student
_____ red	_____ bright	_____ open
_____ window	_____ blue	_____ juice
_____ cold	_____ brother	_____ sad
_____ teacher	_____ class	_____ lawyer
_____ man	_____ tall	_____ room

_____ news   _____ hot   _____ grass

_____ furniture   _____ upstairs   _____ old

_____ moon   _____ green   _____ lazy

_____ bug   _____ woman

*Complete the following sentences using the correct form of the verb **to be**.*

1. My aunt _____ nice.

2. The clouds _____ white.

3. Kathy _____ sick.

4. The ribbons _____ yellow.

5. We _____ twins.

6. The windows _____ open.

7. Colton and Cody _____ brothers.

8. We _____ teachers.

9. It _____ a French book.

10. You _____ very smart.

11. It _____ sad news.

12. She _____ my cousin.

13. You _____ tired.

14. The grass _____ green.

15. It _____ in my room.

16. They _____ lazy.

17. The flower _____ yellow.

18. The bug _____ on the counter.

19. I _____ tall.

20. The man _____ happy.

21. The vacuum _____ red.

22. The tent _____ blue.

23. The juice _____ cold.

24. She _____ a student.

25. They _____ in my class.

26. The woman _____ a lawyer.

27. She _____ upstairs.

28. The teacher _____ smart.

29. The ribbon _____ blue.

30. The water _____ hot.

31. My uncle _____ bald.

32. The furniture _____ old.

33. The fridge _____ in the kitchen.

34. The moon _____ bright.

To Be: Present Tense: Negative Form

Place **not** after the verb **to be** to create the negative form of the present tense.

I am	→	I am not	→	I am not ready.
you are	→	you are not	→	You are not busy.
he is	→	he is not	→	He is not my friend.
she is	→	she is not	→	She is not tall.
it is	→	it is not	→	It is not true.
we are	→	we are not	→	We are not tired.
they are	→	they are not	→	They are not pink.

The negative form of the present tense of the verb **to be** can also be expressed with the contraction **isn't** or **aren't**. There is no contraction for **am not**.

I am not	→	I am not	→	I am not sick.
you are not	→	you aren't	→	You aren't a teacher.
he is not	→	he isn't	→	He isn't a lawyer.
she is not	→	she isn't	→	She isn't ready.
it is not	→	it isn't	→	It isn't a toy.
we are not	→	we aren't	→	We aren't twins.
they are not	→	they aren't	→	They aren't yellow.

EXERCISE

2·1

Use your dictionary to find the meaning of the new vocabulary words needed for this exercise before you begin. Write the words in your language in the space provided.

_____ table	_____ sour	_____ early
_____ city	_____ lime	_____ Spanish
_____ kid	_____ neighbor	_____ drawer
_____ sister	_____ cheese	_____ empty
_____ bus	_____ Italian	_____ pregnant
_____ sister-in-law		

*Rewrite the following sentences to express the negative form. Write the sentence once using **am not**, **is not**, or **are not** and once using the contraction **isn't** or **aren't**.*

1. The cheese is on the table. _____

_____

2. She is my sister. _____

_____

3. My neighbors are Spanish. _____

_____

4. My sister-in-law is Italian. _____

_____

5. Diane is pregnant. _____

_____

6. The limes are sour. _____

_____

7. The bus is empty. _____

_____

8. The kids are early for class today. _____

_____

9. The drawers are empty. _____

_____

10. It is a nice city. _____

_____

EXERCISE
2·2

Use your dictionary to find the meaning of the new vocabulary words needed for this exercise before you begin. Write the words in your language in the space provided.

_____ boss	_____ wife	_____ key
_____ mall	_____ boy	_____ office
_____ far	_____ dragonfly	_____ work
_____ subway	_____ full	_____ garbage can
_____ road	_____ white	_____ garbage bag
_____ eraser	_____ bowl	_____ shelf

_____ fair	_____ black	_____ book
_____ wide	_____ hand	_____ pencil case
_____ husband	_____ pen	_____ school
_____ good	_____ expensive	_____ shoe
_____ idea	_____ late	_____ ceiling
_____ store	_____ car	_____ doctor

Use **am not** or the contraction **isn't** or **aren't** to complete the following negative sentences.

1. The subway _____ full.

2. The windows _____ dirty.

3. It _____ a dragonfly.

4. The keys _____ in the car.

5. The microwave oven _____ in the kitchen.

6. My boss _____ at the office.

7. The boys _____ in the tent.

8. We _____ busy at work.

9. My hands _____ dirty.

10. The eraser _____ in the pencil case.

11. She _____ a teacher in my school.

12. The ceiling _____ white.

13. The bowls _____ on the table.

14. The garbage bags _____ in the drawer.

15. The garbage can _____ full.

16. The store _____ far.

17. It _____ fair.

18. The roads in the city _____ wide.

19. My husband _____ a doctor.

20. The pens _____ black.

21. The books _____ on the shelf.

22. The vacuum _____ in the basement.

23. They _____ friends.

24. The ribbon _____ red.

25. She _____ late for class today.

26. It _____ true.

27. I _____ tired.

28. Barry _____ a good student.

29. The juice _____ cold.

30. My wife _____ at the mall.

31. The shoes _____ expensive.

32. The students _____ tired today

33. The woman _____ old.

34. It _____ a good idea.

To Be: Present Tense: Question Form

Place the verb **to be** before the subject to create the question form of the present tense.

I am	→	am I	→	Am I late?
you are	→	are you	→	Are you my new boss?
he is	→	is he	→	Is he your teacher?
she is	→	is she	→	Is she your neighbor?
it is	→	is it	→	Is it expensive?
we are	→	are we	→	Are we early?
they are	→	are they	→	Are they in the basement?

EXERCISE

3·1

Use your dictionary to find the meaning of the new vocabulary words needed for this exercise before you begin. Write the words in your language in the space provided.

_____ wheel	_____ garage	_____ desk
_____ policeman	_____ French	_____ coat
_____ goldfish	_____ brown	_____ cow
_____ sweet	_____ downstairs	_____ box
_____ meeting	_____ pond	_____ calf
_____ serious	_____ bathroom	_____ frog
_____ English	_____ outside	_____ poor
_____ orange	_____ toothbrush	_____ very
_____ sharpener	_____ toothpaste	
_____ clothesline	_____ bathing suit	

*Rewrite the following sentences to create questions by placing the verb **to be** before the subject. Don't forget to include a question mark (?) in your answer.*

1. The wheels are in the garage. _____

2. The sharpener is on my desk. _____

3. The woman is very poor. _____

4. The toothbrush and toothpaste are in the bathroom. _____

_____

5. My bathing suit is on the clothesline. _____

6. I am in your English class. _____

7. It is cold outside. _____

8. He is a policeman in the city. _____

9. The coats are on the floor. _____

10. Johanne and Véronique are in a meeting. _____

11. The toys are in the box downstairs. _____

12. The cow and calf are brown. _____

13. The orange juice is sweet. _____

14. The frogs are in the pond. _____

15. The goldfish is in the bowl. _____

16. You are serious. _____

17. Marie is French. _____

Use your dictionary to find the meaning of the new vocabulary words needed for this exercise before you begin. Write the words in your language in the space provided.

_____ knife	_____ gate	_____ pot
_____ dishwasher	_____ printer	_____ sheet
_____ fork	_____ nail polish	_____ turkey
_____ bill	_____ bird	_____ Chinese
_____ correct	_____ skunk	_____ Mr.
_____ living room	_____ pillow	_____ Scottish
_____ clean	_____ accountant	_____ needle
_____ real	_____ ink	_____ birdhouse
_____ sharp	_____ fence	_____ pan
_____ lipstick	_____ thread	_____ pig
_____ oven	_____ curtain	_____ garden
_____ bed	_____ pen	_____ again
_____ funny	_____ Mrs.	_____ there
_____ pearl		

Complete the following questions using the correct form of the verb **to be**.

1. _____ it cold in Canada?

2. _____ the skunks in my garden again?

3. _____ the needle and thread in the drawer?

4. _____ he a good accountant?

5. _____ they in the living room?

6. _____ the ink in the printer?

7. _____ the pots and pans clean?

8. _____ she your sister-in-law?

9. _____ the forks in the dishwasher?

10. _____ we ready?

11. _____ it a black pen?

12. _____ I nice?

13. _____ you busy today?

14. _____ the gate open?

15. _____ the fridge empty?

16. _____ Mr. and Mrs. Yee Chinese?

17. _____ the pillows on the bed?

18. _____ the fence white?

19. _____ the books on the shelf?

20. _____ the sheets on the clothesline?

21. _____ the curtains blue?

22. _____ the nail polish purple?

23. _____ the pearls real?

24. _____ Mrs. McMahon Scottish?

25. _____ the turkey in the oven?

26. _____ the birds in the birdhouse?

27. _____ the pigs in the pen?

28. _____ the knife sharp?

29. _____ the bill correct?

30. _____ the lipstick red or pink?

31. _____ they there?

32. _____ I funny?

4·
To Be: Past Tense

The past tense of the verb *to be* is created by using **was** or **were** in place of **am**, **is**, and **are**.

I am	→	I was	→	I was tired at school today.
you are	→	you were	→	You were downstairs.
he is	→	he was	→	He was funny.
she is	→	she was	→	She was at work.
it is	→	it was	→	It was on the shelf.
we are	→	we were	→	We were upstairs.
they are	→	they were	→	They were here.

EXERCISE
4·1

Use your dictionary to find the meaning of the new vocabulary words needed for this exercise before you begin. Write the words in your language in the space provided.

_____ snake	_____ bucket	_____ exam
_____ diaper	_____ pocket	_____ thick
_____ sorry	_____ farm	_____ pool
_____ beach	_____ minnow	_____ washer
_____ pencil	_____ crust	_____ dryer
_____ bag	_____ grandmother	
_____ roommate	_____ hairdresser	
_____ laundry room		

Rewrite the following sentences to create the past tense by changing the present tense form of the verb **to be** *to the past tense form.*

1. Joanie and Isabelle are at the beach. _____

2. He is my roommate. _____

3. It is in my pocket. _____

4. The snake is in the garden. _____

5. The diapers are in the bag. _____

6. She is a hairdresser. _____

7. Lisa is sick. _____

8. The kids are in the pool. _____

9. The bucket is full of minnows. _____

10. The washer and dryer are in the laundry room. _____

11. I am in my office. _____

12. The pencil is on the floor. _____

13. Sorry that I am late. _____

14. The flowers are for Jennifer. _____

15. My grandmother is in the hospital. _____

16. The exam is easy. _____

17. The crust is very thick. _____

18. The farm is very far. _____

Use your dictionary to find the meaning of the new vocabulary words needed for this exercise before you begin. Write the words in your language in the space provided.

_____ huge	_____ cupboard	_____ downtown
_____ ring	_____ asleep	_____ broken
_____ crib	_____ skating rink	_____ godmother
_____ story	_____ slipper	_____ yesterday
_____ fresh	_____ wedding	_____ candle
_____ soft	_____ egg	_____ nurse
_____ spicy	_____ shower	_____ bedroom
_____ baby	_____ awake	_____ last night
_____ with	_____ vase	_____ couch
_____ wine	_____ locker	_____ both
_____ cellar	_____ soup	_____ library
_____ rake	_____ whale	_____ cafeteria

Complete the following past tense sentences using **was** *or* **were**.

1. The baby _____ in the crib.

2. The candles _____ on the table.

3. It _____ a good story.

4. They _____ awake.

5. My godmother _____ asleep on the couch.

6. The wine _____ in the cellar.

7. I _____ ready.

8. He _____ in the shower.

9. The bowls _____ in the cupboard.

10. The girls _____ at the skating rink.

11. The moon _____ bright last night.

12. The juice _____ fresh.

13. The eggs _____ on the counter.

14. My sister _____ outside.

15. The keys _____ in the car.

16. The ring _____ expensive.

17. You _____ at the wedding.

18. The soup _____ hot and spicy.

19. Both pillows _____ soft.

20. Annie _____ a nurse.

21. The flowers _____ in the vase.

22. The rake _____ in the garage.

23. My slippers _____ in the bedroom.

24. The whale _____ huge.

25. We _____ downtown yesterday.

26. Chris _____ in the cafeteria with Cory.

27. It _____ in my locker.

28. We _____ at the library.

29. The pool _____ small.

30. The printer _____ broken.

31. My pockets _____ full.

32. The teachers _____ in the office.

To Be: Past Tense: Negative Form

Place **not** after the past tense form of the verb **to be** to create a negative sentence.

I was	→	I was not	→	I was not sick yesterday.
you were	→	you were not	→	You were not at the beach.
he was	→	he was not	→	He was not at the meeting.
she was	→	she was not	→	She was not very nice.
it was	→	it was not	→	It was not on my desk.
we were	→	we were not	→	We were not late.
they were	→	they were not	→	They were not ready.

The negative form of the past tense of the verb **to be** can also be expressed with the contraction **wasn't** or **weren't**.

I was not	→	I wasn't	→	I wasn't tired last night.
you were not	→	you weren't	→	You weren't at work today.
he was not	→	he wasn't	→	He wasn't serious.
she was not	→	she wasn't	→	She wasn't here yesterday.
it was not	→	it wasn't	→	It wasn't true.
we were not	→	we weren't	→	We weren't at the library.
they were not	→	they weren't	→	They weren't busy last night.

EXERCISE

5·1

Use your dictionary to find the meaning of the new vocabulary words needed for this exercise before you begin. Write the words in your language in the space provided.

_____ dress		_____ waitress		_____ joke
_____ purple		_____ fast		_____ plate
_____ tree		_____ list		_____ play (n)
_____ raccoon		_____ year		_____ name

*Rewrite the following sentences to express the negative form. Write the sentence once using **was not** or **were not** and once using the contraction **wasn't** or **weren't**.*

1. The dress was blue. _____

_____

2. The couch in the living room was dirty. _____

_____

3. They were very fast. _____

_____

4. It was a good joke. _____

_____

5. The raccoons were in the tree. _____

_____

6. The slippers were purple. _____

_____

7. We were at the play last night. _____

_____

8. The plates were in the dishwasher. _____

_____

9. Karen was a waitress for three years. _____

_____

10. My name was on the list. _____

_____

Use your dictionary to find the meaning of the new vocabulary words needed for this exercise before you begin. Write the words in your language in the space provided.

_____ phone	_____ stove	_____ movie
_____ quiet	_____ cat	_____ powder
_____ mark	_____ ugly	_____ stain
_____ clever	_____ slide	_____ funeral
_____ landlord	_____ horn	_____ Greek
_____ butter	_____ sock	_____ polite
_____ deep	_____ long	_____ vegetable
_____ loud	_____ big	_____ snowstorm
_____ jam	_____ lake	_____ light

_____ off   _____ toolbox   _____ hammer

_____ binder   _____ ground   _____ bread

_____ shaver   _____ stroller   _____ museum

_____ nest   _____ rat   _____ on

_____ right answer

Use the contraction **wasn't** *or* **weren't** *to complete the following negative sentences.*

1. My marks _____ good at school last year.

2. It _____ a raccoon; it was a skunk.

3. The stain on the floor _____ big.

4. The vegetables _____ fresh.

5. You _____ very polite with the landlord.

6. It _____ the right answer.

7. The horn in my car _____ loud.

8. We _____ at the funeral.

9. The kids _____ quiet today in class.

10. The grass _____ long.

11. She _____ very clever.

12. The lake _____ deep.

13. The baby _____ in the stroller.

14. He _____ on the slide.

15. My socks _____ on the clothesline.

16. The shaver _____ in the bathroom.

17. The bread and butter _____ on the counter.

18. The museum _____ very big.

19. The rats _____ in the cellar.

20. The nest _____ on the ground.

21. I _____ on the phone.

22. It _____ a big snowstorm.

23. The binders _____ in my locker.

24. The man _____ Greek; he was Italian.

25. The jam _____ in the fridge.

26. It _____ a good movie.

27. The lights _____ on.

28. The stove _____ off.

29. It _____ ugly.

30. The cat _____ black.

31. The hammer _____ in the toolbox.

32. The powder _____ on the shelf.

To Be: Past Tense: Question Form

·6·

Place **was** or **were** before the subject to form questions in the past tense of the verb **to be**.

I was	→	was I	→	Was I funny?
you were	→	were you	→	Were you awake?
he was	→	was he	→	Was he very tall?
she was	→	was she	→	Was she downtown?
it was	→	was it	→	Was it on the floor?
we were	→	were we	→	Were we fast?
they were	→	were they	→	Were they asleep?

EXERCISE

6·1

Use your dictionary to find the meaning of the new vocabulary words needed for this exercise before you begin. Write the words in your language in the space provided.

_____	recipe	_____	crutches	_____	tablecloth
_____	ship	_____	ashtray	_____	bitter
_____	free	_____	sky	_____	seasick
_____	angry	_____	easy	_____	behind
_____	low	_____	velvet	_____	together
_____	door	_____	enough	_____	airplane
_____	lady	_____	nail clippers		
_____	thin	_____	kindergarten		
_____	young	_____	flight attendant		

Rewrite the following sentences to create questions in the past tense by placing **was** *or* **were** *before the subject. Don't forget to include a question mark (?) in your answer.*

1. It was free. _____

2. The airplane was very low in the sky. _____

3. The mall was empty. _____

4. They were in kindergarten together. _____

5. It was bitter. _____

6. You were angry at Susan. _____

7. The recipe was easy. _____

8. The nail clippers were in the drawer. _____

9. The curtains were velvet. _____

10. The tablecloth was dirty. _____

11. It was enough. _____

12. She was a flight attendant when she was young. _____

_____

13. The ashtrays were full. _____

14. The lady was thin. _____

15. Claude was seasick on the ship. _____

16. The crutches were behind the door. _____

6·2

Use your dictionary to find the meaning of the new vocabulary words needed for this exercise before you begin. Write the words in your language in the space provided.

_____ plastic	_____ warm	_____ awful
_____ rotten	_____ high school	_____ snowflake
_____ swan	_____ deodorant	_____ every day
_____ teller	_____ bank	_____ instructions
_____ cashier	_____ blanket	_____ new
_____ after	_____ weather	_____ report card
_____ jar	_____ boring	_____ open
_____ rib	_____ water	_____ pumpkin
_____ marker	_____ ripe	_____ fruit
_____ result	_____ on fire	_____ high chair
_____ snow	_____ driveway	_____ president
_____ iron	_____ parking lot	_____ brush
_____ teddy bear	_____ laptop computer	
_____ grocery store	_____ hardware store	

Complete the following sentences using **was** *or* **were** *to form questions in the past tense.*

1. _____ the weather awful?

2. _____ the snowflakes big?

3. _____ he at school every day?

4. _____ you a cashier at the grocery store?

5. _____ the movie boring?

6. _____ the vegetables fresh?

7. _____ your report card good?

8. _____ the jars on the shelf?

9. _____ the laptop computer new?

10. _____ the teddy bear in the crib?

11. _____ the fruit in the bowl ripe?

12. _____ the baby in the high chair?

13. _____ you in my class in high school?

14. _____ the hardware store open?

15. _____ the ribs good?

16. _____ the swan white?

17. _____ the blankets warm?

18. _____ Sandra on the phone?

19. _____ they at the museum?

20. _____ the pumpkins rotten?

21. _____ the brush in the bathroom?

22. _____ the house on fire?

23. _____ the results good?

24. _____ the driveway full of snow?

25. _____ the iron hot?

26. _____ he the president?

27. _____ the water cold?

28. _____ the deodorant in the bathroom?

29. _____ Linda a teller at the bank?

30. _____ the parking lot full?

31. _____ the instructions in the plastic bag?

32. _____ the marker yellow?

Exceptional Uses with the Verb *To Be*

7·

The following are common expressions that use the verb ***to be***.

to be cold	to be hungry	to be twenty-five years old
to be hot	to be thirsty	to be scared/afraid
to be right	to be wrong	to be ashamed

EXERCISE
7·1

Use your dictionary to find the meaning of the new vocabulary words needed for this exercise before you begin. Write the words in your language in the space provided.

_____ because		_____ daughter		_____ race	
_____ snowball		_____ birthday		_____ son	
_____ mother		_____ breakfast		_____ size	
_____ behavior		_____ thunder		_____ guest	
_____ spider		_____ please		_____ last	
_____ lightning		_____ father		_____ dark	
_____ all the time		_____ this morning			

*Rewrite the following sentences using the correct form of the verb **to be**. Use the information in parentheses at the end of each sentence to help you determine the correct tense and to know whether the sentence is affirmative or negative.*

1. My daughter (to be) afraid of the dark. (present tense, affirmative)

   _____

2. (To be) Jason right? (present tense, affirmative)

   _____

3. She (to be) hungry for breakfast this morning. (past tense, negative)

   _____

4. Please open the windows. I (to be) very hot. (present tense, affirmative)

_____

5. I (to be) ashamed of the size of my shoes. (present tense, negative)

_____

6. Cathy (to be) thirty-three years old on her last birthday. (past tense, affirmative)

_____

7. We (to be) very thirsty after the race. (past tense, affirmative)

_____

8. You (to be) wrong again. (present tense, affirmative)

_____

9. I (to be) right all the time. (present tense, negative)

_____

10. (To be) you scared of thunder? (present tense, affirmative)

_____

11. He (to be) afraid of the lightning. (past tense, negative)

_____

12. I (to be) cold this morning. (past tense, affirmative)

_____

13. (To be) the guests hungry? (present tense, affirmative)

_____

14. My mother and father (to be) ashamed of my behavior. (past tense, affirmative)

_____

15. (To be) your son scared of spiders? (present tense, affirmative)

_____

16. I (to be) eighteen years old. (present tense, negative)

_____

17. Bill is happy because he (to be) right. (present tense, affirmative)

_____

18. I (to be) cold because of the snowballs in my pocket. (present tense, affirmative)

_____

Use your dictionary to find the meaning of the new vocabulary words needed for this exercise before you begin. Write the words in your language in the space provided.

_____ needle _____ shark _____ summer

_____ never _____ jellyfish _____ usually

_____ crow _____ frequently

Complete the following sentences using the correct form of the verb **to be**.

1. He _____ ashamed of you. (past tense, negative)

2. _____ they cold at the beach? (past tense, affirmative)

3. She _____ right. (present tense, negative)

4. We _____ wrong. (past tense, affirmative)

5. Sharon _____ twenty-two years old today. (present tense, affirmative)

6. It _____ hot last summer. (past tense, affirmative)

7. Mark _____ afraid of needles. (present tense, negative)

8. I _____ hungry all the time. (present tense, affirmative)

9. The baby _____ thirsty. (present tense, negative)

10. He _____ wrong. (present tense, affirmative)

11. _____ she right? (past tense, affirmative)

12. It _____ cold in Canada in the winter. (present tense, affirmative)

13. _____ you scared of sharks? (present tense, affirmative)

14. _____ it hot in your class yesterday? (past tense, affirmative)

15. _____ it cold outside? (past tense, affirmative)

16. They _____ wrong. (past tense, negative)

17. She _____ ashamed of her son. (present tense, negative)

18. _____ you cold? (past tense, affirmative)

19. I _____ twenty-two years old. (past tense, negative)

20. They _____ ashamed of her. (present tense, negative)

21. Marcel _____ right. (present tense, affirmative)

22. _____ Ben thirsty? (past tense, affirmative)

23. The boys _____ hungry. (present tense, negative)

24. I _____ scared of jellyfish. (present tense, affirmative)

25. The girls _____ thirsty. (present tense, affirmative)

26. _____ they ashamed of me? (past tense, affirmative)

27. It _____ afraid of you. (past tense, negative)

28. Lucy _____ usually right. (present tense, affirmative)

29. He _____ scared of crows. (present tense, negative)

30. It _____ cold downstairs. (past tense, affirmative)

31. She _____ frequently wrong. (present tense, affirmative)

32. _____ Peter hungry? (present tense, affirmative)

33. I _____ afraid of the frog. (past tense, negative)

34. We _____ very hungry. (present tense, affirmative)

Adjectives

Adjectives are used to describe nouns. They are placed before the noun.

| a *little* dog | a *clean* house | a *nice* neighbor | a *good* friend |
| a *pink* flower | a *busy* man | a *good* recipe | a *blue* bucket |

Adjectives never take *-s* even if the noun is plural.

| *brown* cows | *big* snowflakes | *expensive* cars | *clean* floors |
| *young* girls | *pretty* ribbons | *dirty* shoes | *soft* pillows |

EXERCISE

8·1

Use your dictionary to find the meaning of the following verbs and vocabulary words needed for this exercise before you begin. Write the words in your language in the space provided.

_____ hard	_____ to drink	_____ to see
_____ little	_____ to want	_____ to look
_____ test	_____ leather	_____ windy
_____ cute	_____ hairy	_____ beautiful
_____ prune	_____ for sale	_____ country
_____ handsome		

Rewrite the following sentences, and include the adjective(s) in the correct place in each sentence.

1. The house is for sale. (cute, little) _____

2. It is a knife. (very, sharp) _____

3. He is a man. (tall, handsome) _____

4. It was a day yesterday. (cold, windy) _____

5. I want a jacket. (black, leather) _____

6. They drink juice every morning. (prune) _____

7. The bug is in my shoe. (big, green) _____

8. Elizabeth is a teacher. (French) _____

9. The spider is in the kitchen. (ugly, hairy) _____

10. Canada is a country. (big, beautiful) _____

11. The test was hard. (English) _____

12. He was a policeman. (nice) _____

13. Look at the snow. (beautiful, white) _____

14. The frog is in the pond. (little, green) _____

15. It was a whale. (huge) _____

EXERCISE
8·2

Use your dictionary to find the meaning of the following verbs and vocabulary words needed for this exercise before you begin. Write the words in your language in the space provided.

_____ to make   _____ to wear   _____ to love

_____ to hate   _____ to need   _____ to draw

_____ to like   _____ to watch

_____ pie   _____ right   _____ rhubarb

_____ silver   _____ cake   _____ Mexican

_____ star   _____ BBQ   _____ picture

_____ watch   _____ knee   _____ identical

_____ junk   _____ wealthy   _____ strawberry

_____ sore   _____ dessert   _____ yogurt

_____ food   _____ swollen   _____ round

_____ balloon   _____ left   _____ chocolate

Rewrite the following sentences and include the adjective(s) in the correct place in the sentence.

1. It was a winter. (long, hard) _____

2. I need a watch. (new, silver) _____

3. My hand is sore. (right) _____

4. I want the balloons. (round) _____

5. We like to watch movies. (old) _____

6. Look at the stars in the sky. (bright) _____

7. I like chips. (BBQ) _____

8. They want cake for dessert. (chocolate) _____

9. I love food. (Mexican) _____

10. He is a lawyer. (wealthy) _____

11. You draw pictures. (funny) _____

12. It was a meeting. (long, boring) _____

13. My knee is swollen. (left) _____

14. The kids like food. (junk) _____

15. We like to make pies. (rhubarb) _____

16. I hate yogurt. (strawberry) _____

17. We wear shoes to school. (white) _____

18. They are twins. (identical) _____

To Have: Present Tense

·9·

Use the following to express the present tense of the verb **to have**.

I have	→	I have a red sharpener.
you have	→	You have a beautiful living room.
he has	→	He has a nice wife.
she has	→	She has a blue toothbrush.
it has	→	It has a small baby.
we have	→	We have a swimming pool.
they have	→	They have a new car.

EXERCISE

9·1

Use your dictionary to find the meaning of the new vocabulary words needed for this exercise before you begin. Write the words in your language in the space provided.

_____ skill	_____ tail	_____ next
_____ bad	_____ lunch	_____ taste
_____ roof	_____ weird	_____ paw
_____ skirt	_____ week	_____ smile
_____ headache	_____ attitude	_____ milk
_____ dandruff	_____ terrible	_____ short
_____ sandwich	_____ sleeping bag	
_____ day off	_____ housekeeper	
_____ eye shadow	_____ peanut butter	

*Rewrite the following sentences using **has** or **have** to form the present tense of the verb* **to have**.

1. He (have, has) a bad attitude. _____

2. The cat (have, has) white paws. _____

3. I (have, has) a peanut butter sandwich for lunch today. _____

_____

4. Maria (have, has) a red velvet skirt. _____

5. We (have, has) a nice landlord. _____

6. Jessica (have, has) a terrible headache. _____

7. We (have, has) a good housekeeper. _____

8. She (have, has) a lot of dandruff. _____

9. Tony (have, has) very good skills. _____

10. The milk (have, has) a weird taste. _____

11. The house (have, has) a green roof. _____

12. It (have, has) a short tail. _____

13. We (have, has) a day off next week. _____

14. I (have, has) a warm sleeping bag. _____

15. My sister (have, has) purple eye shadow. _____

16. You (have, has) a nice smile. _____

EXERCISE

9·2

Use your dictionary to find the meaning of the new vocabulary words needed for this exercise before you begin. Write the words in your language in the space provided.

_____ moose	_____ duck	_____ seat
_____ heartburn	_____ helmet	_____ bedroom
_____ nail	_____ area code	_____ cold (n)
_____ education	_____ purse	_____ rocking chair
_____ kitten	_____ sunflower	_____ skate
_____ mailman	_____ boyfriend	_____ girlfriend
_____ same	_____ motorcycle	_____ duckling
_____ banana	_____ shorts	_____ luggage
_____ antlers	_____ puppy	_____ braid
_____ letter	_____ monkey	_____ mirror
_____ parakeet	_____ kettle	_____ clock radio
_____ scary	_____ licorice	_____ skipping rope

*Complete the following sentences using **has** or **have** to form the present tense of the verb **to have**.*

1. I _____ heartburn.

2. He _____ a black helmet.

3. Karina _____ long braids.

4. We _____ rats in the basement.

5. The monkey _____ a banana.

6. I _____ a mirror in my purse.

7. Jay _____ a fast motorcycle.

8. My cat _____ two orange kittens.

9. My sister _____ a boyfriend.

10. I _____ a clock radio in my bedroom.

11. It _____ leather seats.

12. My aunt _____ a cold.

13. Naomi _____ a skipping rope.

14. Derek and Joe _____ black licorice.

15. We _____ a white fridge.

16. He _____ a bad report card this year.

17. The moose _____ big antlers.

18. Billy _____ blue shorts.

19. We _____ sunflowers in the garden.

20. I _____ a new kettle.

21. The mailman _____ a letter for you.

22. They _____ a new puppy.

23. She _____ white skates.

24. You _____ long nails.

25. The duck _____ seven ducklings.

26. We _____ the same area code.

27. My brother _____ a new girlfriend.

28. She _____ a lot of luggage.

29. He _____ a good education.

30. I _____ a rocking chair in my living room.

31. Nathan _____ a scary movie.

32. Jason _____ a blue parakeet.

To Have: Present Tense: Negative Form

Place **do not** or **does not** before the verb **to have** to create a negative sentence. It is important to note that **have** is always used in the negative form and never **has**.

I have	→	I do not have	→	I do not have a dishwasher.
you have	→	you do not have	→	You do not have a pool.
he has	→	he does not have	→	He does not have a helmet.
she has	→	she does not have	→	She does not have braids.
it has	→	it does not have	→	It does not have white paws.
we have	→	we do not have	→	We do not have milk.
they have	→	they do not have	→	They do not have a daughter.

The negative form of the present tense of the verb **to have** can also be expressed with the contraction **don't** or **doesn't**.

I do not have	→	I don't have	→	I don't have a headache.
you do not have	→	you don't have	→	You don't have a flashlight.
he does not have	→	he doesn't have	→	He doesn't have a pen.
she does not have	→	she doesn't have	→	She doesn't have a lawyer.
it does not have	→	it doesn't have	→	It doesn't have a tail.
we do not have	→	we don't have	→	We don't have a garage.
they do not have	→	they don't have	→	They don't have a computer.

EXERCISE

10·1

Use your dictionary to find the meaning of the new vocabulary words needed for this exercise before you begin. Write the words in your language in the space provided.

_____ surprise	_____ fantastic	_____ nose
_____ bangs	_____ customer	_____ about
_____ straight	_____ clown	_____ few
_____ jewelry	_____ antique	_____ flea
_____ screwdriver	_____ brother-in-law	
_____ snowmobile	_____ satellite dish	

Rewrite the following sentences to create the negative form of the verb **to have**. *Write the sentence once using* **do not** *or* **does not** *and once using the contraction* **don't** *or* **doesn't**.

1. My cat has fleas. _____
   _____

2. We have a satellite dish on the roof. _____
   _____

3. I have a surprise for you. _____
   _____

4. Jimmy has a fast snowmobile. _____
   _____

5. We have many good books about antique jewelry. ___
   _____

6. She has a lot of customers. _____
   _____

7. My brother-in-law has a screwdriver. _____
   _____

8. The clown has a big red nose. _____
   _____

9. I have long straight hair and bangs. _____
   _____

10. She has fantastic news. _____
    _____

EXERCISE
10·2

Use your dictionary to find the meaning of the new vocabulary words needed for this exercise before you begin. Write the words in your language in the space provided.

_____ beard	_____ job	_____ doll
_____ mean	_____ saddle	_____ treadmill
_____ office	_____ firecracker	_____ bookmark
_____ shower	_____ mouse	_____ nail file
_____ landlady	_____ relative	_____ coat
_____ whisker	_____ backyard	_____ soft

_____ fur	_____ curly	_____ diamond
_____ glass	_____ ham	_____ filing cabinet
_____ horse	_____ pet	_____ dandelion
_____ ghost	_____ trunk	_____ keyboard
_____ cell phone	_____ German shepherd	

Complete the following sentences using the contraction **don't** *or* **doesn't** *to create the negative form of the verb* **to have** *in the present tense.*

1. You _____ have curly hair.

2. My aunt _____ have a diamond ring.

3. Jennifer _____ have a doll.

4. He _____ have a ham sandwich.

5. I _____ have a new saddle for my horse.

6. Glenn _____ have a boring job.

7. The boys _____ have firecrackers.

8. We _____ have a big back yard.

9. I _____ have a cell phone.

10. The cat _____ have soft fur.

11. We _____ have relatives in New York.

12. The mouse _____ have long whiskers.

13. Samuel _____ have a new keyboard.

14. I _____ have three pets.

15. Richard _____ have a German shepherd.

16. My car _____ have a big trunk.

17. You _____ have a vacuum.

18. She _____ have a question.

19. I _____ have a nail file in my purse.

20. My boss _____ have a filing cabinet.

21. We _____ have a mean landlady.

22. Derrick _____ have a beard.

23. She _____ have a bookmark for the book.

24. They _____ have a shower in the bathroom.

25. He _____ have a cold.

26. They _____ have a wealthy uncle.

27. I _____ have a fur coat.

28. We _____ have many dandelions in the yard.

29. You _____ have a treadmill in the basement.

30. The teachers _____ have a meeting today.

31. I _____ have a glass of red wine.

32. We _____ have a ghost in the attic.

33. Jason _____ have a car.

34. Sharon _____ have a toothbrush.

11· To Have: Present Tense: Question Form

Place **do** or **does** before the subject to create questions with the verb **to have**. As with the negative form, **have** is used for all persons and never **has**.

I have	→	do I have	→	Do I have good skills for the job?
you have	→	do you have	→	Do you have a headache?
he has	→	does he have	→	Does he have a good report card?
she has	→	does she have	→	Does she have a red binder?
it has	→	does it have	→	Does it have a long tail?
we have	→	do we have	→	Do we have a meeting?
they have	→	do they have	→	Do they have relatives in Montreal?

EXERCISE
11·1

Use your dictionary to find the meaning of the new vocabulary words needed for this exercise before you begin. Write the words in your language in the space provided.

_____ scarf	_____ project	_____ flip-flops
_____ dove	_____ meat loaf	_____ important
_____ lease	_____ pager	_____ everything
_____ rights	_____ same	_____ appointment
_____ tight	_____ deadline	_____ celebration
_____ until	_____ wing	_____ Thanksgiving
_____ Christmas Eve	_____ phone number	

*Rewrite the following sentences to create questions by placing **do** or **does** before the subject. Don't forget to include a question mark (?) in your answer.*

1. You have a pink eraser. _____

2. He has my phone number. _____

3. They have everything they need. _____

4. We have the same scarf. _____

5. I have rights. _____

6. Marissa has green flip-flops. _____

7. You have a huge turkey for Thanksgiving. _____

8. They have a lease until next year. _____

9. It has a funny taste. _____

10. You have two important appointments today. _____

_____

11. The dove has white wings. _____

12. We have a day off next week. _____

13. David has a pager. _____

14. Juanita has a good recipe for meat loaf. _____

15. We have a tight deadline for the project. _____

16. They have a big celebration on Christmas Eve. _____

_____

EXERCISE
11·2

Use your dictionary to find the meaning of the new vocabulary words needed for this exercise before you begin. Write the words in your language in the space provided.

_____ mud	_____ receipt	_____ cousin
_____ tire	_____ noodle	_____ bathrobe
_____ gold	_____ tie	_____ ladybug
_____ claw	_____ show	_____ necklace
_____ glasses	_____ time	_____ bib
_____ manager	_____ dictionary	_____ shirt
_____ leg	_____ tooth	_____ mattress
_____ flat	_____ ant	_____ binoculars
_____ wrong	_____ bruise	_____ gym
_____ Germany	_____ eye	_____ beaver
_____ map	_____ poodle	_____ silk
_____ better	_____ membership	_____ polka dot
_____ marshmallow	_____ fax machine	_____ scar
_____ e-mail address		

Complete the following questions with **do** or **does** to create the question form in the present tense with the verb **to have**.

1. _____ I have lipstick on my tooth?

2. _____ you have a new mattress?

3. _____ Mike have a black tie?

4. _____ the kids have a bag of marshmallows?

5. _____ he have the wrong answer?

6. _____ I have a bruise on my arm?

7. _____ he have a membership for the gym?

8. _____ we have binoculars for the show?

9. _____ the soup have a lot of noodles?

10. _____ it have green eyes?

11. _____ you have a better map of the city?

12. _____ they have a poodle?

13. _____ Carlos have my e-mail address?

14. _____ we have winter tires?

15. _____ the horse have a saddle?

16. _____ it have pink polka dots?

17. _____ she have a silk bathrobe?

18. _____ the beaver have a flat tail?

19. _____ I have a scar on my leg?

20. _____ we have a new manager today?

21. _____ she have a cousin in Germany?

22. _____ you have the receipt in the bag?

23. _____ Shaun have new glasses?

24. _____ I have a ladybug on my shirt?

25. _____ Samantha have a gold necklace?

26. _____ we have ants in the basement?

27. _____ I have mud on my shoes?

28. _____ you have a dictionary?

29. _____ they have a fax machine?

30. _____ you have a bib for the baby?

31. _____ I have the right time?

32. _____ the cat have sharp claws?

The Simple Present Tense

The simple present tense is used when stating general facts or true statements that have no time. Add -*s* to the verb for **he**, **she**, and **it**.

I need	→	I need a new computer.
you need	→	You need a good lawyer.
he needs	→	He needs a roommate.
she needs	→	She needs a blanket.
it needs	→	It needs a lot of work.
we need	→	We need a flashlight.
they need	→	They need a new fridge.

Add -*es* to verbs when using **he**, **she**, and **it** if the verb:

ends with z, s, x, ss, ch, or sh	ends with o	ends with y preceded by a consonant—change the y to i before adding -*es*
I wash the car.	I go to school.	I try very hard.
You wash the car.	You go to school.	You try very hard.
He washes the car.	He goes to school.	He tries very hard.
She washes the car.	She goes to school.	She tries very hard.
It washes the car.	It goes to school.	It tries very hard.
We wash the car.	We go to school.	We try very hard.
They wash the car.	They go to school.	They try very hard.

EXERCISE
12·1

Use your dictionary to find the meaning of the following verbs and vocabulary words needed for this exercise before you begin. Write the words in your language in the space provided.

_____	to amaze	_____	to help	_____	to blush
_____	to cry	_____	to see	_____	to smoke
_____	to guard	_____	to kiss	_____	to flush
_____	to jump	_____	to go	_____	to scratch

_____ village   _____ American   _____ king

_____ toilet   _____ kingdom   _____ every

_____ knight   _____ castle   _____ caramel

_____ cigarette   _____ apple   _____ people

Rewrite the following sentences with the correct form of the simple present tense using the verb in parentheses.

1. He (to smoke) American cigarettes. _____

2. Karen (to blush) when she (to see) that boy. _____

3. I (to love) caramel apple cake. _____

4. He (to cry) like a baby. _____

5. It (to amaze) me. _____

6. It (to jump) very high. _____

7. He (to kiss) all the girls in school. _____

8. My cats (to scratch) the furniture. _____

9. They (to help) many people in the village. _____

10. The knights (to guard) the king and castle in the kingdom. _____

_____

11. He never (to flush) the toilet. _____

EXERCISE

12·2

Use your dictionary to find the meaning of the following verbs and vocabulary words needed for this exercise before you begin. Write the words in your language in the space provided.

_____ to crush   _____ to make   _____ to follow

_____ to spoil   _____ to push   _____ to whisper

_____ to explain   _____ to drive   _____ to carry

_____ to manage   _____ to melt   _____ to owe

_____ to dream   _____ to buy   _____ to earn

_____ to own   _____ to eat   _____ to obey

_____ to do   _____ to fear

_____ paramedic   _____ patient   _____ spring

_____ lemon   _____ rule   _____ local

_____ money	_____ cottage	_____ everywhere
_____ stretcher	_____ tea	_____ Laundromat
_____ carriage	_____ laundry	_____ housework
_____ perfume	_____ child	_____ restaurant
_____ raw	_____ onion	_____ waterfalls
_____ bank	_____ grape	_____ nothing

Complete the following sentences with the correct form of the simple present tense using the verb in parentheses.

1. My teacher _____ (to explain) everything.

2. We _____ (to whisper) in class.

3. He _____ (to crush) grapes to make wine.

4. Lisa _____ (to buy) a lot of perfume.

5. I _____ (to do) the housework for my mother.

6. They _____ (to earn) a lot of money.

7. Linda _____ (to work) downtown.

8. My uncle _____ (to manage) a restaurant.

9. The paramedics _____ (to carry) the patient on a stretcher.

10. You _____ (to owe) me money.

11. My grandmother _____ (to eat) raw onions.

12. He _____ (to fear) nothing.

13. They _____ (to follow) me everywhere.

14. I _____ (to work) in the local bank.

15. She _____ (to drink) tea with lemon.

16. Jessica _____ (to push) the baby in a carriage.

17. He _____ (to spoil) his child.

18. Connie _____ (to dream) about waterfalls.

19. Leo _____ (to drive) to work.

20. My husband _____ (to do) the laundry.

21. She _____ (to go) to the Laundromat every week.

22. We _____ (to own) a cottage in the country.

23. The boys _____ (to obey) the rules in class.

24. The snow _____ (to melt) in the spring.

13· The Simple Present Tense: Negative Form

Place **do not** or **does not** before the verb to create the negative form of the simple present tense. The simple form of the verb is always used. Never add *-s* to **he**, **she**, and **it** in the negative form of the simple present tense.

I wear	→ I do not wear	→	I do not wear orange.
you wear	→ you do not wear	→	You do not wear perfume.
he wears	→ he does not wear	→	He does not wear diapers.
she wears	→ she does not wear	→	She does not wear a watch.
it wears	→ it does not wear	→	It does not wear shoes.
we wear	→ we do not wear	→	We do not wear slippers.
they wear	→ they do not wear	→	They do not wear nail polish.

The negative form of the simple present tense can also be expressed with the contraction **don't** or **doesn't**.

I do not drink	→ I don't drink	→	I don't drink apple juice.
you do not drink	→ you don't drink	→	You don't drink wine.
he does not drink	→ he doesn't drink	→	He doesn't drink lemon juice.
she does not drink	→ she doesn't drink	→	She doesn't drink milk.
it does not drink	→ it doesn't drink	→	It doesn't drink water.
we do not drink	→ we don't drink	→	We don't drink or smoke.
they do not drink	→ they don't drink	→	They don't drink and drive.

EXERCISE 13·1

Use your dictionary to find the meaning of the following verbs and vocabulary words needed for this exercise before you begin. Write the words in your language in the space provided.

_____ to sell   _____ to trust   _____ to snore

_____ to yell   _____ to dislike   _____ to swear

_____ to collect   _____ to believe

_____ meat   _____ fish   _____ coin

_____ giant   _____ several   _____ foreign

_____ language   _____ sewing machine

Rewrite the following sentences to express the negative form of the simple present tense. Write the sentence once using **do not** *or* **does not** *and once using the contraction* **don't** *or* **doesn't**.

1. My husband snores every night. _____

   _____

2. I believe your story about the giant monkeys. _____

   _____

3. Nancy and Yvan collect coins. _____

   _____

4. She speaks several foreign languages. _____

   _____

5. It dislikes fish. _____

   _____

6. Ron swears and yells in class. _____

   _____

7. Sara sells sewing machines. _____

   _____

8. I trust you. _____

   _____

9. We eat meat. _____

   _____

EXERCISE
13·2

Use your dictionary to find the meaning of the following verbs and vocabulary words needed for this exercise before you begin. Write the words in your language in the space provided.

_____	to bother	_____	to study	_____	to iron
_____	to gossip	_____	to travel	_____	to deserve
_____	to live	_____	to listen	_____	to sneeze
_____	to smell	_____	to cook	_____	to forgive
_____	to learn	_____	to cough	_____	to feed
_____	to know	_____	to laugh	_____	to write
_____	to hurt	_____	to belong		
_____	stray	_____	office	_____	well
_____	ponytail	_____	coffee	_____	pancake

_____ hard _____ clothes _____ cotton candy

_____ towel _____ alone _____ cockroach

Complete the following sentences using the contraction **don't** *or* **doesn't** *to create the negative form of the simple present tense.*

1. It _____ work well.

2. We _____ feed the stray cats.

3. I _____ dream a lot.

4. Mark _____ want pancakes for breakfast.

5. I _____ iron my clothes.

6. It _____ bother me.

7. She _____ write to Bob.

8. I _____ cook every night.

9. He _____ listen to me.

10. I _____ travel alone.

11. She _____ know you.

12. It _____ hurt.

13. You _____ deserve that.

14. They _____ like cockroaches.

15. Roger _____ want cotton candy.

16. I _____ owe you money.

17. She _____ sneeze all the time.

18. You _____ drink coffee.

19. It _____ smell good.

20. He _____ cough at night.

21. My dog _____ snore.

22. You _____ laugh a lot.

23. He _____ study very hard.

24. Betty _____ gossip in the office.

25. I _____ forgive you.

26. They _____ learn a lot in class.

27. Glenn _____ live here.

28. It _____ belong to you.

29. I _____ need a towel.

30. Latonya _____ want a ponytail in her hair.

The Simple Present Tense: Question Form

Place **do** or **does** before the subject to create questions in the simple present tense. The simple form of the verb is used when creating questions in the simple present tense.

I dream	→	do I dream	→	Do I dream a lot?
you work	→	do you work	→	Do you work well?
he sees	→	does he see	→	Does he see the clock?
she wears	→	does she wear	→	Does she wear flip-flops?
it hates	→	does it hate	→	Does it hate milk?
we want	→	do we want	→	Do we want a dog?
they own	→	do they own	→	Do they own the house?

EXERCISE
14·1

Use your dictionary to find the meaning of the following verbs and vocabulary words needed for this exercise before you begin. Write the words in your language in the space provided.

_____ to touch	_____ to read	_____ to cost
_____ to scream	_____ to boil	_____ to play
_____ to skate	_____ to put	
_____ mortgage	_____ train	_____ fox
_____ on time	_____ soldier	_____ horror
_____ afternoon	_____ dough	_____ woods
_____ pepper	_____ crown	_____ night
_____ newspaper	_____ hobby	_____ salt
_____ everything		

*Rewrite the following sentences to create the question form of the simple present tense. Place **do** or **does** before the subject and use the simple form of the verb. Don't forget to include a question mark (?) in your answer.*

1. She skates in the morning. _____

2. They boil the vegetables. _____

3. He sleeps in the afternoon. _____

4. The boys play chess at night. _____

5. You pay the mortgage on time. _____

6. She reads the English newspaper. _____

7. They drive to work together. _____

8. It costs $20 to travel by train to the city. _____

9. She screams when she watches horror movies. _____

10. She wants a new hobby. _____

11. The king wears a red velvet crown. _____

12. Bobby plays with toy soldiers. _____

13. You put salt and pepper in the dough. _____

14. Jackie touches everything in my office. _____

15. You see the fox in the woods. _____

EXERCISE
14·2

Use your dictionary to find the meaning of the following verbs and vocabulary words needed for this exercise before you begin. Write the words in your language in the space provided.

_____ to agree	_____ to rent	_____ to dye
_____ to annoy	_____ to fish	_____ to chase
_____ to increase	_____ to feel	_____ to weigh
_____ to disturb	_____ to walk	_____ to snow
_____ to interest	_____ to mix	_____ to park
_____ to participate		

_____ credit card	_____ children	_____ smoke
_____ piggy bank	_____ facecloth	_____ truth
_____ cigar	_____ change	_____ pea
_____ lobster	_____ worm	_____ pound
_____ house	_____ coupon	_____ glove
_____ noise	_____ sick	_____ mushroom
_____ driveway	_____ minimum wage	

*Complete the following sentences using **do** or **does** to create questions in the simple present tense.*

1. _____ he annoy you?
2. _____ you pay with your credit card?
3. _____ it snow in your country?
4. _____ you need change?
5. _____ we agree?
6. _____ the minimum wage increase every year?
7. _____ you need a facecloth?
8. _____ he know the truth?
9. _____ you see the smoke?
10. _____ Chris and Jim rent a house?
11. _____ Joan have black gloves?
12. _____ you feel sick?
13. _____ he park in the driveway?
14. _____ it interest you?
15. _____ they want the coupons?
16. _____ she mix the eggs with the milk?
17. _____ the noise disturb you?
18. _____ the children like peas?
19. _____ they walk to school?
20. _____ your dog chase cats?
21. _____ it weigh twenty pounds?
22. _____ you eat lobster?
23. _____ she have a piggy bank?
24. _____ you fish with worms?
25. _____ Jerry smoke cigars?
26. _____ you dye your hair?
27. _____ they like mushrooms?
28. _____ Leslie participate at school?

Possessive Pronouns

15·

Possessive pronouns are used to show ownership or possession of someone or something. They are placed before the noun.

I	→	my	→	I drink my coffee.
you	→	your	→	You drive your car.
he	→	his	→	He needs his screwdriver.
she	→	her	→	She wears her slippers.
it	→	its	→	It chases its tail.
we	→	our	→	We want our money.
they	→	their	→	They help their kids.

EXERCISE
15·1

Use your dictionary to find the meaning of the following verbs and vocabulary words needed for this exercise before you begin. Write the words in your language in the space provided.

_____ to dress	_____ to burn	_____ to take
_____ to open	_____ to visit	_____ to wash
_____ to keep	_____ to bite	_____ to hide
_____ to lick	_____ to wipe	_____ to forget
_____ master	_____ sleeve	_____ mail
_____ sponge	_____ sailor	_____ stair
_____ under	_____ jewel	_____ carpet
_____ homework	_____ apartment	
_____ submarine		

Rewrite the following sentences by choosing the correct possessive pronoun indicated in parentheses that refers back to the subject pronoun.

1. She visits (their, her) relatives every summer. _____

   _____

2. We hide (our, your) money under the carpet in the master bedroom. ____

   _____

3. They keep (his, their) jewels in a jewelry box. _____

4. I wash (your, my) stairs with a sponge. _____

5. He passes all (our, his) exams. _____

6. She dresses (her, his) dolls in pink. _____

7. I open (my, your) mail after breakfast. _____

8. He bites (my, his) nails. _____

9. We rent (my, our) apartment. _____

10. It licks (its, their) paws. _____

11. I burn (your, my) marshmallows. _____

12. Jeff takes (his, our) pills in the morning. _____

13. The boys forget (my, their) homework every day. _____

_____

14. He wipes (his, her) nose on (my, his) sleeve. _____

15. She dyes (her, your) hair. _____

16. The sailors believe (their, my) new submarine is better. _____

_____

Use your dictionary to find the meaning of the following verbs and vocabulary words needed for this exercise before you begin. Write the words in your language in the space provided.

_____ to ride	_____ to curl	_____ to lace
_____ to fry	_____ to leave	_____ to give
_____ to sail	_____ to argue	_____ to protect
_____ to sell	_____ to cut	_____ to use
_____ to fly	_____ to hang	_____ to demand
_____ to greet		

_____ world	_____ day care	_____ head
_____ boat	_____ footprint	_____ skate
_____ sand	_____ fireman	_____ lawn mower
_____ market	_____ kite	_____ freedom
_____ around	_____ week	_____ curling iron

_____ water   _____ skim   _____ sunglasses

_____ bike   _____ diary   _____ arena

_____ field   _____ boot   _____ fireplace

Complete the sentences using the correct possessive pronoun according to the subject.

1. They sail _____ boat around the world.

2. She fries _____ eggs in butter.

3. We give _____ old clothes to Peter.

4. I ride _____ bike to school.

5. She curls _____ hair with a curling iron.

6. You need _____ dark sunglasses.

7. I lace _____ skates at the arena.

8. It drinks _____ water.

9. We sell _____ vegetables at the market.

10. The fireman wears _____ black boots.

11. The twins love and protect _____ brother.

12. I greet _____ guests.

13. They argue with _____ neighbors.

14. He needs _____ lawyer.

15. We demand _____ rights.

16. He uses _____ lawn mower to cut the grass.

17. I scratch _____ head.

18. She hangs _____ clothes on the clothesline.

19. They clean _____ fireplace every week.

20. I drink _____ tea with skim milk.

21. Laura loves _____ husband.

22. You want _____ freedom.

23. We leave _____ kids at the day care.

24. She writes in _____ diary.

25. He flies _____ kite in the field.

26. I see _____ footprints in the sand.

The Simple Past Tense

The simple past is used to describe an action that happened in the recent past. Follow these rules to create the simple past tense with regular verbs.

Add -ed to the simple form of the verb.

to visit

I visited
you visited
he visited
she visited
it visited
we visited
they visited

Add only -d if the verb ends with e.

to believe

I believed
you believed
he believed
she believed
it believed
we believed
they believed

Delete y and add -ied to the simple form of the verb if the verb ends in y preceded by a consonant.

to cry

I cried
you cried
he cried
she cried
it cried
we cried
they cried

When -ed is added to verbs that end in *d*, pronounce the last syllable separately.

to need

I need-ed
you need-ed
he need-ed
she need-ed
it need-ed
we need-ed
they need-ed

When -ed is added to verbs that end in *t*, pronounce the last syllable separately.

to want

I want-ed
you want-ed
he want-ed
she want-ed
it want-ed
we want-ed
they want-ed

The ending of all other regular verbs is pronounced as one syllable when -ed is added.

to open

I opened
you opened
he opened
she opened
it opened
we opened
they opened

EXERCISE 16·1

Use your dictionary to find the meaning of the following verbs and vocabulary words needed for this exercise before you begin. Write the words in your language in the space provided.

_____ to answer   _____ to reward   _____ to try

_____ to increase   _____ to notice   _____ to lie

| _____ to share | _____ to land | _____ to sign |
| _____ to kill | _____ to dry | _____ to challenge |

_____ hair dryer	_____ ditch	_____ age
_____ upside down	_____ inside out	_____ sweater
_____ snack	_____ another	_____ toad
_____ lease	_____ eel	_____ building

*Rewrite the following sentences in the simple past tense by adding **-ed** or **-ied** to the simple form of the verb in parentheses.*

1. I (to use) my hair dryer to dry my hair. _____

2. We (to try) a new recipe last night. _____

3. Thomas (to answer) the phone. _____

4. I (to notice) that your sweater was inside out. _____

   _____

5. The car (to land) upside down in the ditch. _____

   _____

6. She (to share) her snack with her friends at school yesterday. _____

   _____

7. The minimum wage (to increase) last year. _____

8. Suzanne (to lie) about her age. _____

9. My company (to sign) the lease for our building for another three years. _____

   _____

10. The teacher (to challenge) her students and (to reward) them for their hard work. _____

    _____

11. The eel (to kill) the toad. _____

    _____

Use your dictionary to find the meaning of the following verbs and vocabulary words needed for this exercise before you begin. Write the words in your language in the space provided.

| _____ to destroy | _____ to please | _____ to tidy |
| _____ to describe | _____ to expect | _____ to decide |

_____ to rain	_____ to serve	_____ to obtain
_____ to knock	_____ to deny	_____ to prove
_____ to borrow	_____ to accept	_____ to join
_____ to avoid	_____ to marry	_____ to paint
_____ to move	_____ to arrest	

_____ in-line skates	_____ in detail	_____ door
_____ contract	_____ someone	_____ makeup
_____ lawn	_____ weekend	_____ collision
_____ accident	_____ terms	_____ doctor
_____ everybody	_____ audience	_____ alert
_____ innocent	_____ conditions	_____ appetizer
_____ plain	_____ passport	_____ singer
_____ army	_____ court	_____ police

Complete the sentences using the simple past tense by adding **-ed** *or* **-ied** *to the simple form of these regular verbs.*

1. We _____ (to accept) the terms and conditions of the contract.

2. My brother _____ (to join) the army.

3. My neighbors _____ (to move) to Vancouver.

4. Someone _____ (to knock) on the door.

5. He _____ (to describe) the accident in detail.

6. I _____ (to prove) that I was innocent in court.

7. The man _____ (to deny) everything.

8. Tina _____ (to borrow) my in-line skates.

9. They _____ (to watch) the kids in the pool.

10. She _____ (to use) my makeup.

11. I _____ (to tidy) the house for my mother.

12. It _____ (to rain) all day.

13. My husband _____ (to paint) the bathroom on the weekend.

14. I was alert and I _____ (to avoid) the collision.

15. We _____ (to push) the baby in the carriage.

16. My cousin _____ (to marry) a doctor.

17. The singer _____ (to please) the audience.

18. Your dog _____ (to destroy) my lawn.

19. We _____ (to serve) appetizers to our guests.

20. Mike _____ (to obtain) his passport.

21. The police _____ (to arrest) everybody.

22. We _____ (to order) a plain pizza last night.

23. I _____ (to decide) to learn English.

24. We _____ (to expect) to see you there.

The Simple Past Tense with Irregular Verbs: 1

Some verbs do not use the **-ed** ending to express the past tense. These are irregular verbs, and they have unique past tense forms. They have the same form for all persons in the past tense, and they must be memorized.

to hide (hid)	to drink (drank)	to wear (wore)	to go (went)
I hid	I drank	I wore	I went
you hid	you drank	you wore	you went
he hid	he drank	he wore	he went
she hid	she drank	she wore	she went
it hid	it drank	it wore	it went
we hid	we drank	we wore	we went
they hid	they drank	they wore	they went

EXERCISE

17·1

Use your dictionary to find the meaning of the following irregular verbs and vocabulary words needed for this exercise before you begin. Write the words in your language in the space provided.

_____	to feel	→ felt	_____	to do	→ did
_____	to bite	→ bit	_____	to find	→ found
_____	to blow	→ blew	_____	to fall	→ fell
_____	to shake	→ shook	_____	to cut	→ cut
_____	to tear	→ tore	_____	to break	→ broke
_____	to slide	→ slid	_____	to buy	→ bought
_____	to spend	→ spent	_____	to take	→ took
_____	to teach	→ taught			

_____	honeymoon	_____	dishes	_____	when
_____	earthquake	_____	saw	_____	pants
_____	grandparent	_____	cup	_____	math
_____	toboggan	_____	overseas	_____	after

	Ireland		down		gift
	finger		favorite		ankle
	mountain		high school		

Rewrite the following sentences in the simple past tense using the irregular past tense form of the verb in parentheses.

1. She (to blow) on her soup because it was hot. _____

   _____

2. The house (to shake) a lot during the earthquake. _____

   _____

3. They (to take) the plane and (to spend) their honeymoon overseas. _____

   _____

4. I always (to feel) sick when I was pregnant. _____

5. He (to tear) his pants when he (to fall). _____

6. We (to buy) a nice gift for our grandparents in Ireland. _____

   _____

7. The kids (to slide) down the mountain on their new toboggan. _____

   _____

8. I (to do) the dishes after supper. _____

9. I (to cut) my finger on the sharp saw. _____

10. You (to break) my favorite cup. _____

11. Your dog (to bite) my ankle. _____

12. Karen (to find) a purse at the beach. _____

13. I (to teach) math at the high school last year. _____

EXERCISE
17·2

Use your dictionary to find the meaning of the following irregular verbs and vocabulary words needed for this exercise before you begin. Write the words in your language in the space provided.

	to speak	→	spoke		to draw	→	drew
	to hold	→	held		to leave	→	left
	to pay	→	paid		to swear	→	swore
	to steal	→	stole		to sit	→	sat

_____ to hang → hung _____ to hear → heard

_____ to shoot → shot _____ to see → saw

_____ to begin → began _____ to give → gave

_____ to dig → dug

_____ niece _____ plastic _____ midnight

_____ front _____ broom _____ party

_____ store _____ great _____ stop sign

_____ whistle _____ swing _____ shoplifter

_____ thing _____ speech _____ crossing guard

_____ pantry _____ calculator _____ pink flamingo

_____ bored _____ problem _____ nephew

_____ witch _____ tunnel _____ underground

Complete the following sentences in the simple past tense using the irregular past tense form of the verb indicated in parentheses.

1. The teachers _____ (to speak) about the computer problems in detail.

2. I _____ (to begin) my homework after school.

3. He _____ (to give) money to his niece and nephew for their birthdays.

4. She _____ (to hang) the whistle around her neck.

5. I _____ (to see) the shoplifter in the store.

6. We _____ (to sit) on the swings and talked about many things.

7. Somebody _____ (to steal) my calculator and pencils at school.

8. I _____ (to pay) a lot of money for the plastic pink flamingos on my front lawn.

9. Cheyenne _____ (to draw) a nice picture of a witch on a broom.

10. David _____ (to swear) in class today.

11. The workers _____ (to dig) a big underground tunnel.

12. The crossing guard _____ (to hold) the stop sign in her left hand.

13. The police _____ (to shoot) the man in the leg.

14. We _____ (to hear) your speech last night, and it was great.

15. They _____ (to leave) the party at midnight because they were bored.

16. We _____ (to see) a mouse in the pantry last night.

The Simple Past Tense with Irregular Verbs: 2

Some verbs do not use the **-ed** ending to express the past tense. These are irregular verbs, and they have unique past tense forms. They have the same form for all persons in the past tense, and they must be memorized.

Use your dictionary to find the meaning of the following irregular verbs and vocabulary words needed for this exercise before you begin. Write the words in your language in the space provided.

_____ to lend	→	lent	_____ to freeze	→	froze
_____ to have	→	had	_____ to catch	→	caught
_____ to drive	→	drove	_____ to beat	→	beat
_____ to come	→	came	_____ to ride	→	rode
_____ to wake	→	woke	_____ to bend	→	bent
_____ to build	→	built	_____ to sleep	→	slept
_____ to forget	→	forgot		
_____ to understand	→	understood		
_____ to withdraw	→	withdrew		

_____ bacon	_____ cheese	_____ enough
_____ stamp	_____ bullfrog	_____ tadpole
_____ rifle	_____ hanger	_____ envelope
_____ sheep	_____ hunter	_____ post office
_____ hay	_____ lamb	_____ sand castle
_____ first	_____ bagel	_____ warehouse
_____ lunch	_____ month	_____ inventory
_____ barn	_____ whole	_____ lettuce

Rewrite the following sentences in the simple past tense using the irregular past tense form of the verb in parentheses.

1. We (to withdraw) enough money for the whole month. _____
   _____

2. I (to catch) a bullfrog and four tadpoles in the pond. _____
   _____

3. Salina (to ride) a horse for the first time yesterday. _____
   _____

4. Robert, Claire, and Daniel (to build) a huge sand castle on the beach. _____
   _____

5. Brandon (to bend) the hanger to open the car door. _____
   _____

6. I (to drive) to the post office to buy some stamps and envelopes. _____
   _____

7. The hunter (to forget) his rifle in the woods. _____

8. You (to wake) your grandmother when you knocked on the window. _____
   _____

9. The sheep and lamb (to sleep) on the hay in the barn. _____
   _____

10. I (to have) a bagel with bacon, tomato, cheese, and lettuce for lunch. _____
    _____

11. Camilie (to understand) what the teacher taught in class today. _____
    _____

12. My mother (to freeze) the vegetables for the winter. _____
    _____

13. Dimitri (to lend) the shovel to his neighbor. _____

14. The red team (to beat) the blue team. _____

15. Laurent (to come) to help us with the inventory in the warehouse. _____
    _____

Use your dictionary to find the meaning of the following irregular verbs and vocabulary words needed for this exercise before you begin. Write the words in your language in the space provided.

	to shut	→	shut		to keep	→	kept
_____	to bring	→	brought	_____	to rise	→	rose
_____	to win	→	won	_____	to mean	→	meant
_____	to send	→	sent	_____	to hurt	→	hurt
_____	to choose	→	chose	_____	to put	→	put
_____	to grow	→	grew	_____	to lose	→	lost
_____	to cost	→	cost	_____	to think	→	thought
_____	to forgive	→	forgave				

	package		bride		nail
_____	cookie	_____	gardener	_____	screw
_____	early	_____	hearing aid	_____	even though
_____	toe	_____	deaf	_____	gift certificate
_____	cauliflower	_____	hand	_____	weed
_____	gorgeous	_____	airmail	_____	as
_____	joke	_____	umbrella	_____	groom
_____	park	_____	blind	_____	cabbage

Complete the following sentences in the simple past tense using the irregular past tense form of the verb indicated in parentheses.

1. I _____ (to bring) my umbrella when we went for a walk in the park.

2. It _____ (to cost) a lot, but it was gorgeous and we loved it.

3. The sun _____ (to rise) early this morning.

4. He _____ (to win) a gift certificate at the Christmas party.

5. We _____ (to grow) cabbages, cauliflowers, and pumpkins in our garden last summer.

6. The gardener _____ (to put) the weeds in the garbage can.

7. I _____ (to mean) that as a joke.

8. Jasmin _____ (to shut) the door on her toe.

9. The bride and groom _____ (to choose) a beautiful wedding cake.

10. Even though he lied, she _____ (to forgive) him.

11. I _____ (to think) you liked peas.

12. Sharon is blind and deaf, and she _____ (to lose) her hearing aid.

13. It _____ (to hurt) when the cat scratched my hand.

14. My father _____ (to keep) the nails and screws in jars in the garage.

15. He _____ (to send) the package by airmail.

16. We _____ (to drink) milk with our cookies.

The Simple Past Tense with Irregular Verbs: 3

Some verbs do not use the -*ed* ending to express the past tense. These are irregular verbs, and they have unique past tense forms. They have the same form for all persons in the past tense, and they must be memorized.

Use your dictionary to find the meaning of the following irregular verbs and vocabulary words needed for this exercise before you begin. Write the words in your language in the space provided.

	to meet	→	met		to spin	→	spun
	to sing	→	sang		to feed	→	fed
	to ring	→	rang		to fight	→	fought
	to throw	→	threw		to light	→	lit
	to run	→	ran		to eat	→	ate
	to get	→	got		to fit	→	fit
	to know	→	knew		to read	→	read
	to sell	→	sold				

	fire		Monday		Sunday
	too		Tuesday		Wednesday
	ice		concert		Thursday
	Friday		phone		evening
	crime		middle		Saturday
	paper		guilty		icing
	noisy		raise (n)		liquor store
	parrot		out of control		
	power failure				

Rewrite the following sentences in the simple past tense using the irregular past tense form of the verb in parentheses.

1. She (to sing) on Monday, Wednesday, and Friday at the concert in Montreal. _____
   _____

2. The house was dark because of the power failure, so we (to light) the candles. _____
   _____

3. The car (to spin) out of control on the ice. _____

4. I (to read) the newspaper in the evening on Saturday and Sunday. _____
   _____

5. My son (to fight) at school on Tuesday and Thursday last week. _____
   _____

6. The phone (to ring) in the middle of the night. _____
   _____

7. I (to know) that he was guilty of the crime. _____

8. She (to meet) Sara at the liquor store. _____

9. Sorry, but I (to eat) all the icing on your cake when you went to the bathroom. _____
   _____

10. I (to get) a big raise at work last month. _____

11. We (to sell) our parrot because he was too noisy. _____
    _____

12. Alexandre (to throw) the papers in the fire. _____

13. My pants (to fit) me last year. _____

14. Carmen (to run) and hid under the bed. _____

15. We (to feed) meat to the fox. _____

EXERCISE
19·2

Use your dictionary to find the meaning of the following verbs and vocabulary words needed for this exercise before you begin. Write the words in your language in the space provided.

_____	to swim	→	swam	_____	to write	→	wrote
_____	to say	→	said	_____	to sweep	→	swept
_____	to tell	→	told	_____	to stand	→	stood
_____	to hit	→	hit	_____	to deal	→	dealt

_____ to stick → stuck   _____ to make → made

_____ to lead → led   _____ to quit → quit

_____ to fly → flew   _____ to become → became

_____ to weep → wept

_____ sidewalk   _____ glue   _____ chalk

_____ dentures   _____ dolphin   _____ piece

_____ wall   _____ issue (n)   _____ blackboard

_____ date   _____ truth   _____ drink (n)

_____ snowman   _____ stream   _____ housecoat

_____ minute   _____ princess   _____ on vacation

_____ corner   _____ jury

Complete the following sentences in the simple past tense using the irregular past tense form of the verb indicated in parentheses.

1. He _____ (to deal) with many issues at work yesterday.

2. I thought you _____ (to say) it was free.

3. Liliane _____ (to sweep) the sidewalk with her new broom.

4. The kindergarten class _____ (to make) a snowman this morning.

5. I _____ (to stick) the pieces of wood together with glue.

6. I _____ (to hit) my head on the wall when I fell down the stairs.

7. My father _____ (to become) angry when I _____ (to quit) school last year.

8. My grandmother _____ (to wear) her dentures for her date with Mr. Olsen.

9. I _____ (to lead) my horse to the stream for a drink of cold water.

10. We _____ (to fly) the kite in the field all day.

11. The teacher _____ (to write) on the blackboard with pink chalk.

12. Emy and Meghan _____ (to swim) with dolphins when they were on vacation in Florida.

13. The princess _____ (to weep) alone in her room.

14. She says that she _____ (to tell) the truth to the jury.

15. I _____ (to stand) on the corner in the rain and waited for you for twenty minutes.

16. He _____ (to give) me a housecoat and a puppy for my birthday.

The Simple Past Tense: Negative Form

Place **did not** after the subject and use the simple form of the verb to create the negative form of the simple past tense for regular and irregular verbs.

I did not	→	I did not break	→	I did not break the cup.
you did not	→	you did not answer	→	You did not answer me.
he did not	→	he did not believe	→	He did not believe you.
she did not	→	she did not pass	→	She did not pass her test.
it did not	→	it did not jump	→	It did not jump on me.
we did not	→	we did not sell	→	We did not sell our house.
they did not	→	they did not touch	→	They did not touch it.

The negative form of the simple past tense can also be expressed with the contraction **didn't**.

I did not boil	→	I didn't boil	→	I didn't boil the eggs.
you did not build	→	you didn't build	→	You didn't build your house.
he did not want	→	he didn't want	→	He didn't want coffee.
she did not do	→	she didn't do	→	She didn't do her homework.
it did not cost	→	it didn't cost	→	It didn't cost a lot.
we did not sign	→	we didn't sign	→	We didn't sign it.
they did not find	→	they didn't find	→	They didn't find their cat.

EXERCISE
20·1

Use your dictionary to find the meaning of the following verbs and vocabulary words needed for this exercise before you begin. Write the words in your language in the space provided.

_____ to shave   _____ to apologize

_____ to waste   _____ to report

_____ bottle   _____ medicine   _____ clam

_____ screen   _____ valuable   _____ income

_____ skin   _____ mussels

65

Rewrite the following sentences to express the negative form of the simple past tense. Write the sentence once using **did not** *and once using the contraction* **didn't**.

1. They watched the hockey game on their new big-screen TV. _____

_____

2. I forgot to tell him. _____

_____

3. She wasted my valuable time. _____

_____

4. Marcia reported her income. _____

_____

5. I shook the bottle of medicine. _____

_____

6. My uncle shaved his head. _____

_____

7. He apologized to his friend. _____

_____

8. We found clams and mussels in the sand on the beach. _____

_____

9. The police read the man his rights. _____

_____

10. It scratched my skin. _____

_____

EXERCISE
20·2

Use your dictionary to find the meaning of the following verbs and vocabulary words needed for this exercise before you begin. Write the words in your language in the space provided.

_____ to translate   _____ to prevent   _____ to last

_____ to deposit   _____ to express   _____ to save

_____ to gain   _____ to brush

_____ inch   _____ opinion   _____ litter box

_____ wallet   _____ mitten   _____ grandson

	hat		antenna		leftovers
	shower		pipe		pantyhose
	upstairs		Greece		horoscope
	pay		plumber		granddaughter
	trip		savings account		

*Rewrite the following sentences in the negative form using the contraction **didn't** and the simple form of the verb.*

1. He prevented the accident. _____

2. She expressed her opinion. _____

3. The movie lasted three hours. _____

4. They went to see their granddaughter and grandson. _____

5. They saved a lot of money for their trip to Greece. _____

6. Patricia lost her mittens, scarf, and hat at school. _____

7. Sonia translated the letter. _____

8. I bought a gift for her. _____

9. Mario found a black leather wallet in the snow. _____

10. We put the leftovers in plastic bags. _____

11. I tore my pantyhose. _____

12. I knew you were there. _____

13. He deposited his pay in his savings account. _____

14. The plumber fixed the pipes, shower, and toilet in the bathroom upstairs. _____

15. I cleaned the litter box and brushed the cat this morning. _____

16. I read my horoscope today. _____

17. The wind bent the antenna. _____

18. Laura grew two inches and gained ten pounds last year. _____

The Simple Past Tense: Question Form

Place **did** before the subject to create questions in the simple past tense. The simple form of the verb is always used when creating questions in the simple past tense with regular and irregular verbs.

I ate	→	did I eat	→	Did I eat your sandwich?	
you ate	→	did you eat	→	Did you eat my last cookie?	
he ate	→	did he eat	→	Did he eat his dessert?	
she ate	→	did she eat	→	Did she eat the vegetables?	
it ate	→	did it eat	→	Did it eat the egg?	
we ate	→	did we eat	→	Did we eat everything?	
they ate	→	did they eat	→	Did they eat the meat?	

EXERCISE
21·1

Use your dictionary to find the meaning of the following verbs and vocabulary words needed for this exercise before you begin. Write the words in your language in the space provided.

_____ to weigh _____ to cheat _____ to change

_____ to elect _____ to offend _____ to remain

_____ to escape _____ to indicate

_____ cards _____ prison _____ argument

_____ salad _____ peanut _____ overtime

_____ deer _____ scale _____ squirrel

_____ garlic _____ mind _____ rainbow

_____ fight _____ starfish _____ timesheet

_____ remote control

*Rewrite the following sentences to create questions in the simple past tense by placing **did** before the subject and using the simple form of the verb. Don't forget to include a question mark (?) in your answer.*

1. You saw the beautiful rainbow. _____

2. He offended you when he said that. _____

3. Jessica found a starfish on the beach. _____

4. The squirrel ate the peanuts. _____

5. He shot a deer last weekend. _____

6. I indicated my overtime hours on my timesheet. _____

7. They remained friends after the argument. _____

8. Luke broke the remote control for the TV. _____

9. She changed her mind. _____

10. Brandon cheated when we played cards. _____

11. They weighed the fish on the scale. _____

12. You put garlic in the salad. _____

13. The people elected a new president. _____

14. He escaped from prison. _____

15. It slept under your bed. _____

EXERCISE
21·2

Use your dictionary to find the meaning of the following verbs and vocabulary words needed for this exercise before you begin. Write the words in your language in the space provided.

_____ to load   _____ to appear   _____ to ask

_____ to lock   _____ to attend   _____ to climb

_____ to pick   _____ to convince

_____ sunset   _____ diver   _____ roller-coaster

_____ comb   _____ seafood   _____ earring

_____ arm   _____ maid   _____ chipmunk

_____ apron   _____ tree   _____ ice-cream cone

_____ true   _____ bubble   _____ rattlesnake

_____ thief   _____ wagon   _____ treasure chest

_____ safe   _____ handcuffs

Rewrite the following sentences using **did** and the simple form of the verb to create questions in the simple past tense. Don't forget to include a question mark (?) in your answer.

1. You took a picture of the sunset. _____

2. She locked the safe. _____

3. They attended the funeral. _____

4. Barry ordered seafood. _____

5. The chipmunk climbed the tree. _____

6. They rode the roller-coaster. _____

7. She made the earrings. _____

8. The divers found a treasure chest. _____

9. The baby blew bubbles in the bath. _____

10. They loaded the wagon. _____

11. The rattlesnake bit his arm. _____

12. The policeman put handcuffs on the thief. _____ _____

13. She convinced you. _____

14. You picked a flower for me. _____

15. It appeared to be true. _____

16. You asked a question. _____

17. The maid ironed my apron. _____

18. The dog licked my ice-cream cone. _____

19. She drew a picture of a mermaid. _____

20. Ravi lost his comb. _____

Prepositions: *In and On*  ·22·

Use *in* as a preposition to indicate:

the position or location	**the year of occurrence**
The towels are <u>in the dryer</u>.	We married <u>in 2003</u>.
the months and seasons	**points of the day**
My flower garden is beautiful <u>in the summer</u>.	He left <u>in the afternoon</u>.

location within countries, cities, states, and provinces

She goes to school <u>in Montreal</u>. We had fun <u>in Mexico</u>.
He lives <u>in Ohio</u>. I met him <u>in British Columbia</u>.

Use *on* as a preposition to indicate:

an object supported by a top surface	**the directional position of something**
The cup is <u>on the table</u>.	It's the first door <u>on the left</u>.
a time of occurrence	**a method of transportation**
I worked <u>on the weekend</u>.	I felt sick <u>on the plane</u>.
the means of expression	**the subject of study**
We talked <u>on the phone</u> for two hours.	I have a good book <u>on horses</u>.

EXERCISE
22·1

Rewrite the following sentences correctly by choosing **in** *or* **on**.

1. The garbage can is (in, on) the garage. _____

2. Do you see signs of life (in, on) the moon? _____

3. We will talk about it (in, on) the morning. _____

4. Mark moved here (in, on) 1997. _____

5. Don't throw your empty bottle (in, on) the ground. _____

_____

6. We spent five days (in, on) Paris. _____

7. All the kids start school (in, on) September. _____

8. I will see you (in, on) Saturday. _____

9. They advertised it (in, on) the radio (in, on) California. _____

_____

10. What do you have (in, on) your mouth? _____

11. I saw your picture (in, on) the newspaper (in, on) Ontario. _____

_____

12. It's my birthday (in, on) Tuesday. _____

13. The bathroom is (in, on) the left. _____

14. We went for a ride (in, on) his motorcycle (in, on) the country. _____

_____

15. She presented her project (in, on) trees. _____

Use your dictionary to find the meaning of the new vocabulary words needed for this exercise before you begin. Write the words in your language in the space provided.

_____ economy   _____ eyelash   _____ lid

_____ blister   _____ filling   _____ switch

_____ wart   _____ affairs

*Complete the following sentences with **in** or **on**.*

1. They saw you _____ TV last night.

2. My aunt died _____ August.

3. She lives _____ the city.

4. I wrote an article _____ whales.

5. The people are _____ the ship.

6. We skate _____ the winter.

7. She has a wart _____ her nose.

8. We slept _____ the bus.

9. They divorced _____ 2001.

10. Turn the switch _____ the left.

11. Put the tablecloth _____ the table.

12. It's garbage day _____ Thursday.

13. Do you live _____ Michigan?

14. He became the president _____ 2005.

15. Your breakfast is _____ the tray.

16. I have a little eyelash _____ my eye.

17. The answer is _____ the book.

18. I want to change the carpet _____ my room.

19. The twins were born _____ Alberta.

20. We will buy a new car _____ the spring.

21. The flashlight is _____ the fridge.

22. We like to walk _____ the evening.

23. Who is the man _____ your right?

24. I have a filling _____ my back tooth.

25. Put the lid _____ the jar.

26. It is the best hotel _____ the world.

27. She gave a presentation _____ the economy.

28. We arrived _____ the morning.

29. I have a blister _____ my toe.

30. They work _____ the United States.

31. We have a day off _____ Monday.

32. His report was _____ world affairs.

33. Look at all the snow _____ the roof.

34. She screamed _____ the middle of the night.

35. The fly is _____ the ceiling.

36. She lives _____ Washington.

37. Paul wasn't with me _____ Wednesday.

38. I had lunch _____ the train.

39. Celine will have her baby _____ January.

40. We bought our house _____ 1995.

There Is and There Are: Present Tense

Use **there is** and **there are** to show that something exists. Use **there is** with singular nouns and **there are** with plural nouns.

Singular		Plural
There is a gift for you on the table.	→	There are two gifts for you on the table.
There is a sand castle on the beach.	→	There are a lot of sand castles on the beach.
There is a dove on the fence.	→	There are many doves on the fence.
There is a button on the floor.	→	There are three buttons on the floor.

EXERCISE 23·1

Use your dictionary to find the meaning of the new vocabulary words needed for this exercise before you begin. Write the words in your language in the space provided.

_____ colt	_____ meatball	_____ quilt
_____ sink	_____ gigantic	_____ piglet
_____ rock	_____ peppers	_____ stallion
_____ street	_____ seagull	_____ sauce
_____ caterpillar	_____ fire hydrant	
_____ whiteboard	_____ phone book	

*Rewrite the following sentences by choosing **there is** or **there are** depending on whether the noun is singular or plural.*

1. (There is, There are) many meatballs and red peppers in the sauce.

   _____

2. (There is, There are) a whiteboard in my classroom.

   _____

3. (There is, There are) rocks in my boot.

   _____

4. (There is, There are) a phone book on her desk.

_____

5. (There is, There are) gigantic footprints in the snow.

_____

6. (There is, There are) a fire hydrant at the corner of my street.

_____

7. (There is, There are) many caterpillars on the tree.

_____

8. (There is, There are) a black stallion in the field.

_____

9. (There is, There are) four piglets and three colts in the barn.

_____

10. (There is, There are) a quilt on my bed.

_____

11. (There is, There are) many seagulls on the beach.

_____

12. (There is, There are) a new keyboard in the box.

_____

13. (There is, There are) two sponges in the bucket.

_____

14. (There is, There are) many dirty plates in the sink.

_____

15. (There is, There are) six diamonds on my ring.

_____

16. (There is, There are) a few gray squirrels in the tree.

_____

Use your dictionary to find the meaning of the new vocabulary words needed for this exercise before you begin. Write the words in your language in the space provided.

_____ tow truck	_____ proof	_____ pen
_____ airport	_____ near	_____ downtown
_____ shoulder	_____ cave	_____ tablespoon
_____ dressing	_____ bat	_____ over there
_____ beehive	_____ check	_____ polka dot
_____ ear	_____ gun	_____ several
_____ oil	_____ muffin	_____ long-distance call
_____ sugar	_____ snack	_____ reward
_____ paper clip	_____ bullet	_____ teaspoon
_____ toothpick	_____ wrinkle	_____ forehead
_____ chin	_____ dustpan	_____ freckle
_____ mosquito	_____ raisin	_____ fire extinguisher

Complete the following sentences with **is** or **are** depending on whether the noun directly following the verb is singular or plural.

1. There _____ many stars in the sky.

2. There _____ a beehive in the garage.

3. There _____ enough proof.

4. There _____ a big roller-coaster over there.

5. There _____ several tow trucks downtown.

6. There _____ a small airport outside the city.

7. There _____ a check for you in the mail.

8. There _____ a teaspoon of sugar in my tea.

9. There _____ many bats in the cave.

10. There _____ a box of paper clips in the drawer.

11. There _____ bullets in the gun.

12. There _____ a dustpan in the closet.

13. There _____ spaghetti sauce on your chin.

14. There _____ many wrinkles on your forehead.

15. There _____ a parking lot at the corner.

16. There _____ a long-distance call for you.

17. There _____ three freckles on my nose.

18. There _____ a fire extinguisher in the kitchen.

19. There _____ hunters in the woods.

20. There _____ a dog pen in the backyard.

21. There _____ snacks for everybody.

22. There _____ a big reward for you.

23. There _____ pink polka dots on my dress.

24. There _____ a hardware store near the mall.

25. There _____ many raisins in my muffin.

26. There _____ a mosquito on your shoulder.

27. There _____ a scar on my knee.

28. There _____ two tablespoons of oil in the salad dressing.

29. There _____ a gold earring in his left ear.

30. There _____ a lot of toothpicks in the jar.

There Is and *There Are:* Present Tense: Negative Form

24·

Place *not* after *there is* and *there are* to create a negative sentence.

| there is | → | there is not | → | There is not a rocking chair downstairs. |
| there are | → | there are not | → | There are not many blankets on my bed. |

The negative form of *there is* and *there are* can also be expressed with the contractions *there isn't* and *there aren't*.

| there is not | → | there isn't | → | There isn't a bug in the house. |
| there are not | → | there aren't | → | There aren't many leftovers. |

EXERCISE

24·1

Use your dictionary to find the meaning of the new vocabulary words needed for this exercise before you begin. Write the words in your language in the space provided.

_____ folder	_____ rabbit	_____ cage
_____ shade	_____ tricycle	_____ quarter
_____ log	_____ penny	_____ scarecrow
_____ button	_____ dime	_____ angel
_____ turtle	_____ thermometer	
_____ nickel	_____ wishing well	

Rewrite the following sentences to express the negative form of **there is** *and* **there are**. *Write the sentence once using* **is not** *or* **are not** *and once using the contraction* **isn't** *or* **aren't**.

1. There is a lot of shade in the backyard. _____

   _____

2. There are three gold buttons on my coat. _____

   _____

3. There are two yellow folders on my desk. _____

   _____

4. There is a tricycle on the sidewalk. _____

_____

5. There is a thermometer in the bathroom. _____

_____

6. There are three white rabbits in the cage. _____

_____

7. There is a turtle on the log. _____

_____

8. There are many angels in the picture. _____

_____

9. There is a scarecrow in the field. _____

_____

10. There are many dimes and nickels in the wishing well. _____

_____

11. There are five quarters and a penny in my back pocket. _____

_____

Use your dictionary to find the meaning of the new vocabulary words needed for this exercise before you begin. Write the words in your language in the space provided.

_____ yearbook	_____ wrist	_____ dip
_____ alarm clock	_____ hollow	_____ bracelet
_____ wall	_____ woodpecker	_____ pay phone
_____ ferry	_____ face	_____ passenger
_____ region	_____ cemetery	_____ lock
_____ phone booth	_____ grasshopper	_____ ice cube
_____ knot	_____ flour	_____ sandbox
_____ rubber	_____ rag	_____ cushion
_____ satin	_____ dresser	_____ hole
_____ flight	_____ church	_____ across
_____ tiny	_____ valley	_____ price tag
_____ theater	_____ row	_____ dirt
_____ feather	_____ butterfly	_____ oar

*Use the contraction **isn't** or **aren't** to complete the following negative sentences.*

1. There _____ enough time.

2. There _____ a pay phone in my school.

3. There _____ many grasshoppers in the valley.

4. There _____ a phone booth at the corner.

5. There _____ several chairs in the basement.

6. There _____ a lock on the door.

7. There _____ a skunk in the hollow log.

8. There _____ a cemetery in my town.

9. There _____ many ice cubes in my drink.

10. There _____ a sandbox in the park.

11. There _____ a hole in my pocket.

12. There _____ many rags in the bucket.

13. There _____ a satin cushion on the floor.

14. There _____ two alarm clocks on my dresser.

15. There _____ a butterfly on the flower.

16. There _____ enough noodles in my soup.

17. There _____ a tiny spider on the wall.

18. There _____ many rows in the theater.

19. There _____ dirt on my face.

20. There _____ a knot in the gold necklace.

21. There _____ a price tag on the sweater.

22. There _____ many passengers on this flight.

23. There _____ enough flour for this recipe.

24. There _____ many woodpeckers in my region.

25. There _____ enough dip for the vegetables.

26. There _____ many cars on the ferry.

27. There _____ a bracelet on her wrist.

28. There _____ a church across the street.

29. There _____ many feathers in the pillow.

30. There _____ a picture of you in my yearbook.

31. There _____ oars in the rubber boat.

There Is and *There Are*: Present Tense: Question Form

Place *is* or *are* before *there* to create questions in the present tense.

> there is → is there → Is there a kitten outside?
> there are → are there → Are there ducks in the pond?

EXERCISE

25·1

Use your dictionary to find the meaning of the new vocabulary words needed for this exercise before you begin. Write the words in your language in the space provided.

_____ owl	_____ handle	_____ place mat
_____ alien	_____ catfish	_____ lifeguard
_____ germ	_____ suitcase	_____ life jacket
_____ ruler	_____ UFO	_____ candy cane
_____ vending machine	_____ skyscraper	
_____ measuring cup	_____ diving board	

*Rewrite the following sentences to create questions by placing **is** or **are** before **there**. Don't forget to include a question mark (?) in your answer.*

1. There is a vending machine in the cafeteria. _____

   _____

2. There are enough life jackets in the boat. _____

   _____

3. There are many skyscrapers in the city. _____

4. There is a lifeguard at the pool. _____

5. There are two owls in the tree. _____

6. There is a diving board at the public pool. _____

   _____

7. There are germs on my hands. _____

8. There is a handle on my suitcase. _____

9. There is a UFO in the sky. _____

10. There are aliens in the UFO. _____

11. There are candy canes on the Christmas tree. _____

_____

12. There is a ruler on my desk. _____

13. There are enough place mats on the table. _____

14. There is a measuring cup in the cupboard. _____

15. There is a catfish in the pail. _____

16. There are many hangers in the closet. _____

17. There is a mirror in your purse. _____

EXERCISE

25·2

Use your dictionary to find the meaning of the new vocabulary words needed for this exercise before you begin. Write the words in your language in the space provided.

_____ fishing rod	_____ blister	_____ jail
_____ neighborhood	_____ spinach	_____ walnut
_____ spare	_____ fingerprint	_____ pushpin
_____ corkscrew	_____ heel	_____ can opener
_____ playroom	_____ rooster	_____ trunk
_____ hitchhiker	_____ kennel	_____ butcher
_____ blood	_____ flyswatter	_____ elevator
_____ porcupine	_____ stew	_____ rolling pin
_____ pool table	_____ marble	_____ tire
_____ traffic light		

*Complete the following questions with **is** or **are** depending on whether the noun directly referring to the verb is singular or plural.*

1. _____ there fingerprints on the gun?

2. _____ there a pool table in the playroom?

3. _____ there a porcupine in the yard?

4. _____ there many marbles in the jar?

5. _____ there a rolling pin in the drawer?

6. _____ there a rooster on your farm?

7. _____ there many traffic lights in the city?

8. _____ there a hitchhiker on the road?

9. _____ there a spare tire in the trunk?

10. _____ there two blisters on my heel?

11. _____ there many fishing rods in the boat?

12. _____ there enough marshmallows for me?

13. _____ there a mouse in the house?

14. _____ there blood on your shirt?

15. _____ there three elevators in this building?

16. _____ there a lot of dandelions in the yard?

17. _____ there a fireman at the door?

18. _____ there a can opener on the counter?

19. _____ there meatballs in the stew?

20. _____ there a pushpin on the floor?

21. _____ there clean socks in the drawer?

22. _____ there many dogs in the kennel?

23. _____ there a corkscrew in the drawer?

24. _____ there many parking lots in Montreal?

25. _____ there a phone book in the phone booth?

26. _____ there walnuts in the spinach salad?

27. _____ there a jail in your neighborhood?

28. _____ there icing on the cake?

29. _____ there a fire hydrant near your house?

30. _____ there enough plates for everybody?

31. _____ there baby squirrels in the nest?

32. _____ there a flyswatter in the kitchen?

33. _____ there a broom in the garage?

34. _____ there are many good butchers in the city?

There Is and There Are: Past Tense

The past tense of the singular **there is** is **there was**, and the past tense of the plural **there are** is **there were**. Use **there was** and **there were** to show that something existed in the past.

there is	→ there was →	There was a loud noise downstairs last night.
there are	→ there were →	There were dark clouds in the sky.

EXERCISE
26·1

Use your dictionary to find the meaning of the new vocabulary words needed for this exercise before you begin. Write the words in your language in the space provided.

_____ circle	_____ gravy	_____ stray
_____ west	_____ alley	_____ triangle
_____ rust	_____ east	_____ fireworks
_____ straw	_____ wet	_____ CD player
_____ square	_____ cork	_____ hurricane
_____ south	_____ north	_____ belly button
_____ magnifying glass	_____ mashed potatoes	

*Rewrite the following past tense sentences by choosing **was** or **were** depending on whether the noun directly following the verb is singular or plural.*

1. There (was, were) rust on the knife.

   _____

2. There (was, were) rules to follow.

   _____

3. There (was, were) a big sale at the mall, so I bought a scarf and shoes.

   _____

4. There (was, were) a CD player in my car, but someone stole it.

   _____

5. There (was, were) wet towels on the floor after he took his shower.

   _____

6. There (was, were) a hurricane in the southeast last week.

   _____

7. There (was, were) many stray cats in the alley.

   _____

8. There (was, were) beautiful fireworks in the sky last night.

   _____

9. There (was, were) a magnifying glass on the table.

   _____

10. There (was, were) two circles, three squares, and four triangles in the picture.

   _____

11. There (was, were) a diamond in her belly button.

   _____

12. There (was, were) a cork in the bottle of wine.

   _____

13. There (was, were) many straws in the cup on the counter in the kitchen.

   _____

14. There (was, were) a good story about you in the newspaper this morning.

   _____

15. There (was, were) a lot of dirty pots and pans in the sink.

   _____

16. There (was, were) many dimes, nickels, and quarters in my piggy bank.

   _____

17. There (was, were) gravy on my mashed potatoes but not on my meat.

   _____

18. There (was, were) a snowstorm in the northwest last night.

   _____

Use your dictionary to find the meaning of the new vocabulary words needed for this exercise before you begin. Write the words in your language in the space provided.

_____ lily pad	_____ cheek	_____ flag
_____ commercial	_____ reason	_____ teabag
_____ wax	_____ spiderweb	_____ ladder
_____ stranger	_____ tear	_____ clothespin
_____ priest	_____ teapot	_____ pole
_____ knitting needle	_____ dance	_____ online
_____ pear	_____ windmill	_____ decision
_____ wooden	_____ dew	_____ Mother's Day
_____ calendar	_____ France	_____ guy
_____ in line		

Complete the following past tense sentences using **was** or **were** depending on whether the noun directly following the verb is singular or plural.

1. There _____ a new priest in my church today.

2. There _____ a lot of clothespins in the bag.

3. There _____ many houses for sale last year.

4. There _____ a spiderweb in my truck.

5. There _____ good reasons for his decision.

6. There _____ a wooden ladder in the garage.

7. There _____ many pears in the tree.

8. There _____ a flag on the pole.

9. There _____ three knitting needles in the basket.

10. There _____ a rainbow after the storm.

11. There _____ dew on the grass this morning.

12. There _____ a parade on Mother's Day.

13. There _____ many people online.

14. There _____ four rubber ducks in the bath.

15. There _____ a stranger at the door.

16. There _____ many tourists in France last year.

17. There _____ a calendar on my desk.

18. There _____ two teabags in the teapot.

19. There _____ a car in the ditch.

20. There _____ tears on her cheek.

21. There _____ frogs on the lily pads.

22. There _____ a ghost in the attic.

23. There _____ wax on the table.

24. There _____ someone in the phone booth.

25. There _____ a good commercial on TV.

26. There _____ windmills in the field.

27. There _____ a mosquito in the tent.

28. There _____ many tall guys at the dance.

29. There _____ only one waitress yesterday.

30. There _____ many people in line.

31. There _____ a lot of weeds in the garden.

32. There _____ many accidents this morning.

33. There _____ a power failure last night.

34. There _____ a hockey game on TV last night.

27·
There Is and *There Are*: Past Tense: Negative Form

Place *not* after *there was* and *there were* to create a negative sentence.

| there was | → | there was not | → | There was not a doll on the chair. |
| there were | → | there were not | → | There were not many kids in the pool. |

The negative form of *there was* and *there were* can also be expressed with the contractions *there wasn't* and *there weren't*.

| there was not | → | there wasn't | → | There wasn't a bruise on his arm. |
| there were not | → | there weren't | → | There weren't many fish in the lake. |

EXERCISE
27·1

Use your dictionary to find the meaning of the new vocabulary words needed for this exercise before you begin. Write the words in your language in the space provided.

_____ wreath	_____ desert	_____ game
_____ stone	_____ beaver	_____ camel
_____ dam	_____ crack	_____ peach
_____ hall	_____ shell	_____ heavy
_____ bridge	_____ windshield	
_____ octopus	_____ wheelchair	

Rewrite the following sentences to express the negative form. Write the sentence once using **was not** *or* **were not** *and once using the contraction* **wasn't** *or* **weren't**.

1. There was a crack in my windshield. _____

_____

2. There were many shells and stones in the sand on the beach. _____

_____

3. There were a lot of big heavy trucks on the bridge this morning. _____

_____

_____

4. There was a peach in my lunch box. _____

_____

5. There were two staplers on my desk in my office. _____

_____

6. There was a big brown beaver near the dam. _____

_____

7. There were many wheelchairs in the hall in the hospital. _____

_____

8. There was a wreath on the door. _____

_____

9. There were many camels in the desert. _____

_____

10. There was a huge octopus in the boat. _____

_____

11. There were many fun games to play. _____

_____

EXERCISE
27·2

Use your dictionary to find the meaning of the new vocabulary words needed for this exercise before you begin. Write the words in your language in the space provided.

_____ wicker	_____ shadow	_____ rope
_____ wiener	_____ wallpaper	_____ pickle
_____ zoo	_____ mouthwash	_____ polar bear
_____ breeze	_____ hamburger	_____ stuffing
_____ sign	_____ poison ivy	_____ crumb
_____ cool	_____ bank account	_____ stripe
_____ plenty	_____ sheet of paper	_____ crowd
_____ stable	_____ cinnamon	_____ chapter
_____ ash	_____ live concert	_____ glove compartment
_____ gorilla	_____ bus strike	_____ forest
_____ cub	_____ traffic jam	_____ tuna
_____ lock	_____ hot dog bun	_____ scrambled eggs

Use the contraction **wasn't** *or* **weren't** *to complete the following negative sentences.*

1. There _____ a bottle of mouthwash on the shelf in the bathroom.

2. There _____ many chapters in the book.

3. There _____ a rope in the boat.

4. There _____ scrambled eggs for breakfast.

5. There _____ wallpaper on the wall.

6. There _____ a traffic jam on the highway.

7. There _____ stripes on his shirt.

8. There _____ a tuna sandwich for you.

9. There _____ many signs on the road.

10. There _____ a shadow on the wall.

11. There _____ a map in the glove compartment.

12. There _____ many sheets of paper.

13. There _____ crumbs on the plate.

14. There _____ ink in the printer.

15. There _____ enough pickles on my hamburger.

16. There _____ a bus strike in the city.

17. There _____ a lot of money in her bank account.

18. There _____ plenty of time.

19. There _____ three polar bear cubs.

20. There _____ a teaspoon of cinnamon in the jar.

21. There _____ gorillas at the zoo.

22. There _____ many wicker chairs in the store.

23. There _____ enough wieners for the hot dog buns.

24. There _____ ashes in the fireplace.

25. There _____ a big crowd outside.

26. There _____ stuffing in the turkey.

27. There _____ many horses in the stable.

28. There _____ a live concert on TV last night.

29. There _____ poison ivy in the forest.

30. There _____ a cool breeze last night.

31. There _____ a big ship in the lock.

32. There _____ hunters in the woods.

There Is and *There Are:* Past Tense: Question Form

·28·

Place **was** or **were** before **there** to create questions in the past tense.

| there was | → | was there | → | Was there a cushion on the chair? |
| there were | → | were there | → | Were there enough snacks for the kids? |

EXERCISE

28·1

Use your dictionary to find the meaning of the new vocabulary words needed for this exercise before you begin. Write the words in your language in the space provided.

_____ splinter   _____ bone   _____ outhouse

_____ rose   _____ skull   _____ entrance

_____ rude   _____ dice   _____ fuzzy

_____ thumb   _____ bow   _____ without

_____ room   _____ thorn   _____ locksmith

_____ blind spot   _____ rearview mirror

_____ garage sale   _____ cigarette butt

_____ Canada goose

*Rewrite the following sentences to create questions by placing **was** or **were** before **there**. Don't forget to include a question mark (?) in your answer.*

1. There were many knights to guard the castle in the kingdom.

   _____

2. There was a wooden outhouse behind our cottage in the country.

   _____

3. There was a picture of a skull and bones on the bottle.

   _____

4. There were many cigarette butts in the ashtray.

   _____

5. There was a car in my blind spot.

   _____

6. There were pink fuzzy dice on his rearview mirror.

   _____

7. There was a splinter in his thumb.

   _____

8. There was enough room on the bus for everybody.

   _____

9. There was a rude boy in your class last year.

   _____

10. There were two pretty blue bows in her hair.

    _____

11. There was a Canada goose near the lake.

    _____

12. There was a green carpet on the floor in the entrance.

    _____

13. There was a lot of garlic in the butter.

    _____

14. There were many people without a passport at the airport.

    _____

15. There were many thorns on the rose.

    _____

16. There was a garage sale last weekend.

    _____

17. There were many people on the roller-coaster.

    _____

18. There was a locksmith in the mall.

    _____

Use your dictionary to find the meaning of the new vocabulary words needed for this exercise before you begin. Write the words in your language in the space provided.

_____	ocean	_____	playpen	_____	lane
_____	walrus	_____	playground	_____	ketchup
_____	tusk	_____	anchor	_____	penny
_____	blind	_____	fly	_____	Earth
_____	dime	_____	rusty	_____	fog
_____	oatmeal	_____	dinosaur	_____	bus stop
_____	axe	_____	dimple	_____	pillowcase
_____	olive	_____	prize	_____	cardboard
_____	password	_____	bench	_____	raft
_____	factory				

*Complete the following past tense questions with **was** or **were** depending on whether the noun directly referring to the verb is singular or plural.*

1. _____ there dinosaurs on Earth?

2. _____ there a cardboard box in the bedroom?

3. _____ there a lock on the door?

4. _____ there a manager in the restaurant?

5. _____ there a blind on the window?

6. _____ there a bench in the playground?

7. _____ there a rusty axe in the barn?

8. _____ there many pennies in the jar?

9. _____ there toys in the playpen for the baby?

10. _____ there a fly in the spiderweb?

11. _____ there a motorcycle in the parking lot?

12. _____ there a dime in your pocket?

13. _____ there two olives in your drink?

14. _____ there a pillowcase on the pillow?

15. _____ there a raft on the river?

16. _____ there stars in the sky that night?

17. _____ there enough hangers in the closet?

18. _____ there a prize for me?

19. _____ there many lanes on the highway?

20. _____ there a bus stop at the corner?

21. _____ there many workers in the factory?

22. _____ there a password on your computer?

23. _____ there fog on the lake?

24. _____ there a broken tusk on the walrus?

25. _____ there a satellite dish in the yard?

26. _____ there cute dimples on her cheeks?

27. _____ there a silver earring in his left ear?

28. _____ there a huge anchor on the beach?

29. _____ there many divers in the ocean?

30. _____ there ketchup in the recipe?

31. _____ there a hair dryer in your luggage?

32. _____ there a goldfish in the bowl?

33. _____ there oatmeal cookies in the oven?

34. _____ there tea in the teapot?

Prepositions: To and At ·29·

Use *to* as a preposition to describe a movement or an action toward a person, place, or thing.

I walk to school.　　　　　　　She goes to the bank every week.

Use *at* as a preposition to describe an action performed when a person or thing arrives at a location.

We learn a lot at school.　　　　I hurt my knee at the playground.

Use *at* as a preposition to refer to time.

We have a meeting at three o'clock.　　He eats breakfast at 7:30 A.M.

EXERCISE
29·1

Use your dictionary to find the meaning of the new vocabulary words needed for this exercise before you begin. Write the words in your language in the space provided.

_____ daily 　　_____ opponent 　　_____ core

_____ muzzle 　　_____ bonfire 　　_____ England

_____ press 　　_____ Spain

Rewrite the following sentences correctly by choosing to or at.

1. Please explain this (to, at) me. _____

2. The girls ate cake (to, at) the birthday party. _____

_____

3. We saw Tony and his brother (to, at) the restaurant. _____

_____

4. I sold my car (to, at) Mike. _____

5. I bought a muzzle for my dog (to, at) the pet store. _____

_____

6. The funeral was (to, at) four o'clock. _____

7. We fed the apple cores (to, at) the raccoons. _____

_____

8. I go (to, at) the gym daily. _____

9. We made a bonfire (to, at) the beach. _____

10. They drive (to, at) the city. _____

11. The elevator went (to, at) the basement. _____

12. We noticed that there was a policeman (to, at) the door. _____

_____

13. He talked (to, at) the press after the meeting. _____

14. They gave the prize (to, at) my opponent. _____

15. Call me (to, at) 6:30 P.M. _____

16. We went (to, at) England and Spain last year. _____

EXERCISE
29·2

Use your dictionary to find the meaning of the new vocabulary words needed for this exercise before you begin. Write the words in your language in the space provided.

_____ winner	_____ player	_____ detention
_____ dizzy	_____ cliff	_____ Australia
_____ edge	_____ silk	_____ one-way ticket
_____ nearby	_____ loan	_____ work of art
_____ auction	_____ shore	_____ left-handed
_____ outfit	_____ emerald	_____ troublemaker
_____ race	_____ congratulations	

Complete the following sentences with **to** *or* **at**.

1. I forgot my homework _____ my house.

2. They signed the contract _____ the courthouse.

3. He sent a gift certificate _____ his mother.

4. I felt dizzy _____ school today.

5. We met Bob _____ the airport.

6. Throw it _____ me.

7. The teacher sent the class troublemaker _____ the office.

8. Wait for me _____ the bus stop.

9. Meet me _____ the mall _____ one o'clock.

10. He bought a one-way ticket _____ Australia.

11. We walked _____ the edge of the cliff.

12. The kids jumped off the boat and swam _____ the shore.

13. They stayed _____ a nearby hotel.

14. Congratulations _____ the winner.

15. I lent my silk pants _____ Sylvie.

16. I think she is _____ work.

17. Go _____ bed.

18. She had a detention _____ school yesterday.

19. Linda gave her pink sharpener _____ me.

20. My appointment is _____ 3:30 P.M.

21. Talk _____ me.

22. They bought it _____ the garage sale.

23. The teacher read a story _____ the students.

24. I gave the black glove _____ the left-handed player.

25. She forgot her sweater _____ the day care.

26. They went _____ the bank for a loan.

27. I bought a work of art _____ the auction.

28. We lost a lot of money _____ the horse race.

29. She wore her white outfit _____ the party last night.

30. Mylene left her emerald ring _____ my house.

31. He returned _____ his apartment.

32. Ronald studied _____ McGill University.

33. It starts _____ six o'clock.

34. Happy birthday _____ you!

The Present Progressive (Continuous) Tense

The present progressive is used to describe an activity that is presently in progress. It is formed using the verb *to be* and by adding *-ing* to the simple form of the verb.

I drink	→	I am drinking	→	I am drinking my milk with a straw.
you drink	→	you are drinking	→	You are drinking my wine.
he drinks	→	he is drinking	→	He is drinking a cold beer.
she drinks	→	she is drinking	→	She is drinking a cup of tea.
it drinks	→	it is drinking	→	It is drinking the water in the toilet.
we drink	→	we are drinking	→	We are drinking orange juice.
they drink	→	they are drinking	→	They are drinking grape juice.

EXERCISE
30·1

Use your dictionary to find the meaning of the following verbs and vocabulary words needed for this exercise before you begin. Write the words in your language in the space provided.

_____ to sue	_____ to cross	_____ to shiver
_____ to pour	_____ to howl	_____ to repair
_____ to sew	_____ to worry	_____ to growl
_____ to bark	_____ to discuss	_____ to knit
_____ wolf	_____ hiccup	_____ canoe
_____ mayor	_____ pothole	_____ stadium
_____ Big Dipper	_____ Little Dipper	
_____ soft drink	_____ stepfather	
_____ enormous	_____ goose bump	
_____ groundhog	_____ bulletproof vest	
_____ bleachers	_____ retirement home	

*Rewrite the following sentences in the present progressive tense. Use the correct form of the verb **to be**, and add **-ing** to the simple form of the verb in parentheses.*

1. The wolf (to howl) at the moon. _____

2. Sheila (to worry) now because her daughter is late. _____

_____

3. It is cold. We (to shiver) and we have goose bumps. _____

_____

4. They (to cross) the lake in a canoe. _____

5. The mayor (to discuss) the enormous potholes on the roads. _____

_____

6. She (to pour) a soft drink for you. _____

7. The nuns (to sew) clothes and (to knit) slippers for the children. _____

_____

8. The policeman (to wear) his bulletproof vest. _____

9. My great-grandfather (to live) in a retirement home. _____

_____

10. They (to sue) the city. _____

11. We (to look) at the Big Dipper and the Little Dipper with our binoculars. _____

_____

12. Rollande (to drink) water because she has the hiccups. _____

_____

13. My stepfather (to repair) the bleachers in the stadium. _____

_____

14. It (to snow) again. _____

15. The dog (to bark) and (to growl) at the groundhog outside. _____

_____

Use your dictionary to find the meaning of the following verbs and vocabulary words needed for this exercise before you begin. Write the words in your language in the space provided.

_____ to overflow _____ to chew _____ to rub

_____ to juggle _____ to rattle _____ to drool

_____ to wave _____ to tickle _____ to rewind

_____ to surround _____ to tease _____ to deliver

_____ dentist _____ flyer _____ queen

_____ high heels _____ poverty _____ postcard

_____ back _____ filling _____ godfather

_____ law _____ ball _____ treat

Complete the following sentences to form the present progressive tense. Use the correct form of the verb **to be**, *and add* **-ing** *to the simple form of the verb in parentheses.*

1. She _____ (to dress) the baby in the bedroom.

2. You _____ (to cough) a lot.

3. She _____ (to tickle) me.

4. I _____ (to rewind) the movie.

5. The queen _____ (to wave) at the crowd.

6. He _____ (to rub) my back.

7. The baby _____ (to drool) again.

8. They _____ (to sit) in the dining room.

9. Many people _____ (to live) in poverty.

10. Robin _____ (to deliver) flyers to the houses.

11. They _____ (to write) on their desks.

12. She _____ (to whisper) in my ear.

13. You _____ (to break) the law.

14. Someone _____ (to ring) the bell.

15. My team _____ (to win).

16. The windows _____ (to rattle).

17. He _____ (to tease) the dog.

18. You _____ (to annoy) me.

19. Karen _____ (to curl) her hair.

20. You _____ (to waste) my time.

21. The clown _____ (to juggle) the balls.

22. The toilet upstairs _____ (to overflow).

23. Your dog _____ (to chew) on your high heels.

24. The dentist _____ (to put) a filling in my tooth.

25. I _____ (to send) a postcard to my godfather.

26. The police _____ (to surround) the building.

27. I _____ (to leave) now.

28. Randy _____ (to draw) a picture for his friend.

29. The ice cubes _____ (to melt) in my glass.

30. I _____ (to give) the dog a treat.

The Present Progressive (Continuous) Tense: Negative Form

Place **not** after the verb **to be** to create the negative form of the present progressive tense.

I am following	→ I am not following	→ I am not following you.
you are following	→ you are not following	→ You are not following him.
he is following	→ he is not following	→ He is not following a recipe.
she is following	→ she is not following	→ She is not following the rules.
it is following	→ it is not following	→ It is not following me.
we are following	→ we are not following	→ We are not following the car.
they are following	→ they are not following	→ They are not following us.

The negative form of the present progressive tense can also be expressed with the contraction **isn't** or **aren't**. There is no contraction for **am not**.

I am not washing	→	→ I am not washing the floor.
you are not washing	→ you aren't washing	→ You aren't washing your hair.
he is not washing	→ he isn't washing	→ He isn't washing his hands.
she is not washing	→ she isn't washing	→ She isn't washing the dishes.
it is not washing	→ it isn't washing	→ It isn't washing its baby.
we are not washing	→ we aren't washing	→ We aren't washing our car.
they are not washing	→ they aren't washing	→ They aren't washing the dog.

EXERCISE
31·1

Use your dictionary to find the meaning of the following verbs and vocabulary words needed for this exercise before you begin. Write the words in your language in the space provided.

_____ to plant   _____ to sink   _____ to bury

_____ to shout   _____ to wait   _____ to cheer

_____ to stir   _____ to clap

_____ seat belt   _____ seed   _____ paintbrush

_____ elementary

*Rewrite the following sentences to create the negative form of the present progressive tense. Write your answer once with **am not**, **is not**, or **are not** and once with the contraction **isn't** or **aren't**.*

1. He is shouting at you. _____

_____

2. They are waiting downstairs for us. _____

_____

3. The ship is sinking. _____

_____

4. The dog is burying the bone in the sand. _____

_____

5. We are planting the seeds in the garden. _____

_____

6. I am teaching in the elementary school this year. _____

_____

7. Mike is stirring the paint with the paintbrush. _____

_____

8. You are wearing your seat belt. _____

_____

9. The crowd is clapping and cheering. _____

_____

EXERCISE
31·2

Use your dictionary to find the meaning of the following verbs and vocabulary words needed for this exercise before you begin. Write the words in your language in the space provided.

_____ to separate	_____ to stare	_____ to wink
_____ to wiggle	_____ to bore	_____ to free
_____ to joke	_____ to sharpen	_____ to swallow
_____ to invite	_____ to drip	_____ to complain
_____ to surrender	_____ to star	_____ to pray
_____ to dance	_____ to solve	_____ to wrap
_____ to end	_____ to correct	

_____ coleslaw   _____ puzzle   _____ yolk

_____ real estate agent _____ egg white   _____ grapefruit

_____ thief   _____ cabbage roll   _____ buffalo

_____ scissors   _____ tap   _____ relationship

_____ horseshoe   _____ present   _____ puddle

_____ hostage

Use **am not** or the contraction **isn't** or **aren't** to complete the following sentences in the negative present progressive form. Add **-ing** to the simple form of the verb in parentheses.

1. She _____ (to joke) about that.

2. They _____ (to pray) in the church.

3. We _____ (to dance) together.

4. I _____ (to make) cabbage rolls and coleslaw.

5. He _____ (to put) horseshoes on his horse.

6. The taps _____ (to drip) in the bathroom.

7. It _____ (to wiggle) in the box.

8. We _____ (to walk) in the puddle.

9. My mother _____ (to squeeze) the grapefruit.

10. I _____ (to separate) the yolk and egg white.

11. We _____ (to end) our relationship.

12. The teacher _____ (to correct) the exams.

13. We _____ (to complain).

14. It _____ (to bore) me.

15. He _____ (to aim) his rifle at the buffalo.

16. Ronald and Lee _____ (to solve) the puzzle.

17. My real estate agent _____ (to work) hard.

18. I _____ (to star) in a movie.

19. He _____ (to wink) at you.

20. They _____ (to free) the hostages.

21. The thief _____ (to surrender) to the police.

22. We _____ (to wrap) the presents.

23. The woman _____ (to swallow) the medicine.

24. He _____ (to sharpen) the scissors.

25. The secretary _____ (to type) a letter.

26. We _____ (to invite) the neighbors.

The Present Progressive (Continuous) Tense: Question Form

·32·

Place the verb **to be** before the subject to create questions in the present progressive tense.

I am watching	→	am I watching	→	Am I watching you?
you are watching	→	are you watching	→	Are you watching the game?
he is watching	→	is he watching	→	Is he watching the news?
she is watching	→	is she watching	→	Is she watching the time?
it is watching	→	is it watching	→	Is it watching me?
we are watching	→	are we watching	→	Are we watching them?
they are watching	→	are they watching	→	Are they watching the kids?

EXERCISE

32·1

Use your dictionary to find the meaning of the following verbs and vocabulary words needed for this exercise before you begin. Write the words in your language in the space provided.

_____ to enjoy	_____ to slice	_____ to bleed
_____ to sweat	_____ to rock	_____ to offer
_____ to talk	_____ to add	
_____ saleslady	_____ deal	_____ sunrise
_____ newborn	_____ bow	_____ pineapple
_____ suburb	_____ lip	_____ expense
_____ compass	_____ arrow	_____ forward
_____ backward	_____ business trip	
_____ gas station	_____ employee	

*Rewrite the following sentences to create the question form of the present progressive tense by placing the verb **to be** before the subject. Don't forget to include a question mark (?) in your answer.*

1. They are talking about the newborn baby.

   _____

2. He is hunting with a bow and arrow.

   _____

3. The saleslady is offering you a good deal.

_____

4. It is walking backward or forward.

_____

5. The employees are adding their expenses for the business trip.

_____

6. Mrs. Smith is living in the suburbs.

_____

7. Mr. Jones is working in a gas station.

_____

8. He is slicing the pineapple.

_____

9. I am rocking the boat.

_____

10. She is sweating a lot.

_____

11. My lip is bleeding.

_____

12. You are bringing your compass when we go in the woods.

_____

13. Bob and Tina are on the beach enjoying the sunrise.

_____

14. I am eating your muffin.

_____

15. Rosa is making a cake for the surprise birthday party.

_____

EXERCISE
32·2

Use your dictionary to find the meaning of the following verbs and vocabulary words needed for this exercise before you begin. Write the words in your language in the space provided.

_____ to crawl   _____ to burst   _____ to wag

_____ to shuffle   _____ to fail   _____ to show

_____ to spy   _____ to grate   _____ to suffer

_____ to sob   _____ to kid   _____ to throw up

_____ grater   _____ science   _____ wheelbarrow

_____ leaf   _____ bagpipes   _____ breadboard

_____ wave   _____ maple   _____ crusty bread

_____ snail   _____ seal   _____ water wings

Rewrite the following sentences to create questions in the present progressive tense by placing the verb **to be** _before the subject._

1. Tom is spying on us. _____

2. He is pushing the kids in the wheelbarrow. _____

3. The patient is suffering a lot. _____

4. She is cutting the crusty bread on the breadboard. _____

   _____

5. Jimmy is throwing up in the bathroom. _____

6. I am failing my science class. _____

7. Roger is playing the bagpipes. _____

8. The children are bursting the balloons. _____

9. The little boy is showing me something. _____

10. The snail is crawling on the tree. _____

11. Shane is drawing a maple leaf. _____

12. The seals are playing in the waves. _____

13. They are swimming in the pool with their water wings. _____

    _____

14. Chris is grating the cheese with the grater. _____

15. They are kidding. _____

16. He is shuffling the cards. _____

17. Grace is sobbing in her bedroom. _____

18. The dog is wagging its tail. _____

The Past Progressive (Continuous) Tense

The past progressive is used to describe an activity that happened and continued for a period of time in the past. It is formed using the past tense of the verb **to be** and by adding **-ing** to the simple form of the verb.

I am using	→	I was using	→	I was using the stove.
you are using	→	you were using	→	You were using my stapler.
he is using	→	he was using	→	He was using my car.
she is using	→	she was using	→	She was using my makeup.
it is using	→	it was using	→	It was using its paws.
we are using	→	we were using	→	We were using the glue.
they are using	→	they were using	→	They were using the laptop.

EXERCISE 33·1

Use your dictionary to find the meaning of the following verbs and vocabulary words needed for this exercise before you begin. Write the words in your language in the space provided.

_____ to enter	_____ to cover	_____ to roll
_____ to lower	_____ to change	_____ to talk
_____ to test	_____ to divide	_____ to ram
_____ to drop	_____ to place	_____ to glow
_____ shock	_____ tollbooth	_____ music
_____ tour	_____ distance	_____ during
_____ wig	_____ disease	_____ AIDS
_____ lightbulb	_____ christening	
_____ snowshoe	_____ up-to-date	
_____ headphones	_____ laboratory	
_____ Grand Canyon		

Rewrite the following sentences to form the past progressive tense. Use the correct past tense form of the verb **to be**, *and add* **-ing** *to the simple form of the verb in parentheses.*

1. The laboratory (to test) the blood for AIDS and other diseases.

   _____

2. We (to walk) in the snow with our snowshoes.

   _____

3. The mechanic (to lower) the car when it fell.

   _____

4. The girls (to talk) on the phone for two hours.

   _____

5. I (to change) the lightbulb when I got a shock.

   _____

6. The kids (to roll) down the mountain.

   _____

7. She (to place) a wig on her head when I entered.

   _____

8. George (to listen) to music with his headphones.

   _____

9. Vance (to cover) his answers during the test.

   _____

10. We (to buy) a gift for the christening.

   _____

11. I (to drop) a quarter in the tollbooth when he rammed the back of my car.

   _____

12. My daughter (to blow) her nose.

   _____

13. The lights (to glow) in the distance.

   _____

14. They (to struggle) to keep the files up-to-date.

   _____

15. We (to divide) our time between the Grand Canyon and the casinos.

   _____

Use your dictionary to find the meaning of the following verbs and vocabulary words needed for this exercise before you begin. Write the words in your language in the space provided.

_____ to weave	_____ to scold	_____ to warn
_____ to welcome	_____ to grieve	_____ to gamble
_____ to comb	_____ to crush	_____ to bloom
_____ to hatch	_____ to act	_____ to reach
_____ janitor	_____ can	_____ drops
_____ parlor	_____ raincoat	_____ tights
_____ pork	_____ widower	_____ recess
_____ label	_____ memo	_____ tablet
_____ hostess	_____ spoon	_____ bean
_____ railroad	_____ mask	_____ spark
_____ widow	_____ goal	_____ bulletin board
_____ strange	_____ nuts	_____ everywhere

Complete the following sentences to form the past progressive tense. Use the correct past tense form of the verb **to be***, and add* **-ing** *to the simple form of the verb in parentheses.*

1. The flowers _____ (to bloom) in the garden.

2. Réal _____ (to eat) pork and beans.

3. Sam _____ (to crush) the tablets with a spoon.

4. The old man _____ (to warn) us.

5. The hostess _____ (to welcome) our guests.

6. I _____ (to put) the memo on the bulletin board.

7. We _____ (to wear) our raincoats.

8. The kids _____ (to play) ball during recess.

9. The squirrels _____ (to hide) the nuts in the backyard.

10. I _____ (to read) the label on the can.

11. Manon _____ (to wear) white tights.

12. I _____ (to talk) to my boss in his office.

13. They _____ (to cry) at school today.

14. The widow _____ (to grieve) for a long time.

15. They _____ (to weave) baskets.

16. I _____ (to comb) my hair.

17. She _____ (to scold) her children.

18. My father _____ (to work) on the railroad.

19. You _____ (to frighten) the kids with that scary mask on your face.

20. My uncle _____ (to gamble) all night.

21. The sparks _____ (to fly) everywhere.

22. The widower _____ (to act) strange at the funeral parlor.

23. We _____ (to reach) our goals.

24. Suzanne _____ (to sweep) the sidewalk.

25. The eggs _____ (to hatch).

26. I _____ (to put) drops in my eyes.

The Past Progressive (Continuous) Tense: Negative Form

Place **not** after the past tense form of the verb **to be** to create the negative form of the past progressive tense.

I was moving	→ I was not moving	→ I was not moving my leg.
you were moving	→ you were not moving	→ You were not moving it.
he was moving	→ he was not moving	→ He was not moving his pen.
she was moving	→ she was not moving	→ She was not moving her lips.
it was moving	→ it was not moving	→ It was not moving its tail.
we were moving	→ we were not moving	→ We were not moving our car.
they were moving	→ they were not moving	→ They were not moving it.

The negative form of the past progressive tense can also be expressed with the contraction **wasn't** or **weren't**.

I was not helping	→ I wasn't helping	→ I wasn't helping him.
you were not helping	→ you weren't helping	→ You weren't helping me.
he was not helping	→ he wasn't helping	→ He wasn't helping his aunt.
she was not helping	→ she wasn't helping	→ She wasn't helping the nurse.
it was not helping	→ it wasn't helping	→ It wasn't helping us.
we were not helping	→ we weren't helping	→ We weren't helping her.
they were not helping	→ they weren't helping	→ They weren't helping them.

EXERCISE
34·1

Use your dictionary to find the meaning of the following verbs and vocabulary words needed for this exercise before you begin. Write the words in your language in the space provided.

_____ to nip _____ to choke _____ to succeed

_____ to smile

_____ side _____ cancer _____ course

_____ collar _____ stomach _____ treatment

_____ lung _____ chemotherapy

*Rewrite the following sentences to create the negative form of the past progressive tense. Write your answer once with **was not** or **were not** and once with the contraction **wasn't** or **weren't**.*

1. She was getting chemotherapy treatments for lung cancer. _____

   _____

2. My stomach was growling in class this morning. _____

   _____

3. We were driving on the wrong side of the road. _____

   _____

4. He was smiling at you. _____

   _____

5. It was nipping my ankle. _____

   _____

6. The collar was choking the dog. _____

   _____

7. Tania was succeeding in her course and she quit. _____

   _____

8. The guests were eating the potato salad. _____

   _____

9. They were joking. _____

   _____

EXERCISE
34·2

Use your dictionary to find the meaning of the following verbs and vocabulary words needed for this exercise before you begin. Write the words in your language in the space provided.

_____ to count	_____ to pet	_____ to dive
_____ to taste	_____ to overdo	_____ to drip
_____ to snip	_____ to hover	_____ to distract
_____ to carve	_____ to flap	_____ to slur
_____ to cope	_____ to rot	_____ to rely
_____ to breathe		

_____ officer	_____ speech	_____ wire
_____ word	_____ donkey	_____ artist

	teeth		lampshade		welfare
	shotgun		chick		helicopter
	dock		underwear		undercover
	grease		escalator		gingerbread
	wing		dental floss		

Complete the following sentences using the contraction **wasn't** *or* **weren't** *to complete the following sentences in the negative past progressive form. Add* **-ing** *to the simple form of the verb in parentheses.*

1. He _____ (to snip) the black wire.

2. The officer _____ (to work) undercover.

3. You _____ (to overdo) it.

4. The man _____ (to rely) on welfare.

5. The hunter _____ (to carry) a shotgun.

6. We _____ (to make) a gingerbread house.

7. The artist _____ (to carve) the wood.

8. She _____ (to cope) with it very well.

9. He _____ (to slur) his words.

10. They _____ (to dive) in your pool.

11. I _____ (to taste) your dessert.

12. We _____ (to feed) the ducks.

13. I _____ (to clean) my teeth with dental floss.

14. The bird _____ (to flap) its wings.

15. You _____ (to distract) me during my speech.

16. The grease _____ (to drip) on the floor.

17. He _____ (to wear) a lampshade on his head.

18. We _____ (to sit) on the dock.

19. They _____ (to jump) on the escalator.

20. The apples _____ (to rot) on the ground.

21. The helicopter _____ (to hover) over my house.

22. The little girl _____ (to pet) the donkey.

23. We _____ (to count) the baby chicks.

24. He _____ (to wear) clean underwear.

25. She _____ (to breathe).

26. They _____ (to laugh).

The Past Progressive (Continuous) Tense: Question Form

Place the past tense form of the verb **to be** before the subject to create questions in the past progressive tense.

I was swimming	→ was I swimming	→ Was I swimming well?
you were swimming	→ were you swimming	→ Were you swimming alone?
he was swimming	→ was he swimming	→ Was he swimming with you?
she was swimming	→ was she swimming	→ Was she swimming at night?
it was swimming	→ was it swimming	→ Was it swimming in the bath?
we were swimming	→ were we swimming	→ Were we swimming better?
they were swimming	→ were they swimming	→ Were they swimming fast?

EXERCISE

35·1

Use your dictionary to find the meaning of the following verbs and vocabulary words needed for this exercise before you begin. Write the words in your language in the space provided.

_____ to drift	_____ to crack	_____ to grab
_____ to heal	_____ to attract	_____ to dust
_____ to thaw	_____ to guide	_____ to float
_____ to hope	_____ to stop	
_____ to rehearse		

_____ bull	_____ vitamin	_____ horn
_____ snorkel	_____ attention	_____ actor
_____ wound	_____ nightgown	_____ sea
_____ body	_____ pregnancy	_____ match
_____ peacock	_____ watermelon	
_____ goggles	_____ corn on the cob	

Rewrite the following sentences to create the question form of the past progressive tense by placing **was** *or* **were** *before the subject. Don't forget to include a question mark (?) in your answer.*

1. The police were stopping everyone at the corner.

   _____

2. My yellow rubber duck was floating in the bath.

   _____

3. The meat was thawing on the counter.

   _____

4. The wounds on his body were healing.

   _____

5. She was hoping for a new nightgown for Christmas.

   _____

6. The ice was cracking on the lake.

   _____

7. The beautiful peacock was attracting a lot of attention.

   _____

8. She was buying watermelon and corn on the cob for the picnic.

   _____

9. The actors were rehearsing for the play.

   _____

10. It was drifting on the sea.

    _____

11. They were using matches to light the candles on the cake.

    _____

12. You were swimming with goggles and a snorkel.

    _____

13. Réal was grabbing the bull by the horns.

    _____

14. She was taking vitamins during her pregnancy.

    _____

15. The housekeeper was dusting the furniture.

    _____

Use your dictionary to find the meaning of the following verbs and vocabulary words needed for this exercise before you begin. Write the words in your language in the space provided.

_____ to measure	_____ to pretend	_____ to dare
_____ to investigate	_____ to close	_____ to pant
_____ to rip	_____ to start	_____ to spit
_____ to omit	_____ to beg	_____ to raise
_____ crime	_____ detail	_____ cart
_____ barefoot	_____ detective	_____ elbow
_____ ox	_____ pebble	_____ goat
_____ waist	_____ hip	_____ ape

*Rewrite the following sentences to create questions in the past progressive tense by placing **was** or **were** before the subject. Don't forget to include a question mark (?) in your answer.*

1. She was starting her car. _____

2. They were begging us to stay for supper. _____

3. We were closing the store early. _____

4. They were walking barefoot on the pebbles. _____

5. The dog was panting. _____

6. You were scratching your elbow. _____

7. She was measuring her waist and hips. _____

8. Danny was daring me to jump in the lake. _____

9. It was eating my peanut butter sandwich. _____

10. You were ripping my sweater. _____

11. Gary was omitting the details. _____

12. It was following me. _____

13. The detectives were investigating the crime. _____

14. He was spitting on the sidewalk. _____

15. They were raising goats. _____

16. You were pretending to be a big ape. _____

17. I was reading the right letter. _____

18. The ox was pulling the cart. _____

Prepositions: *From and Of*

36·

Use *from* as a preposition to:

indicate a starting point of a movement

We drove <u>from Montreal to Toronto</u>.

measure between points

I work <u>from 8:00 A.M. to 4:00 P.M.</u>

indicate a starting point of an action

My husband called me <u>from work</u>.

indicate the source

She got the information <u>from John</u>.

Use *of* as a preposition to:

indicate the cause or reason of an action

He died <u>of a heart attack</u>.

indicate belonging

I met the <u>queen of England</u>.

describe a characteristic of a person

He is a <u>man of great courage</u>.

indicate the contents

I drank two <u>cups of coffee</u> this morning.

EXERCISE
36·1

Use your dictionary to find the meaning of the new vocabulary words needed for this exercise before you begin. Write the words in your language in the space provided.

_____ talent   _____ beyond   _____ value

_____ bouquet

*Rewrite the following sentences correctly by choosing **from** or **of**.*

1. We gave her a beautiful bouquet (from, of) flowers.

   _____

2. I got a toothbrush (from, of) my dentist.

   _____

3. He is a member (from, of) the hockey hall (from, of) fame.

   _____

4. She sent me a postcard (from, of) Canada.

_____

5. Peter is a man (from, of) many talents.

_____

6. We heard voices (from, of) beyond the bushes.

_____

7. He called me (from, of) a pay phone.

_____

8. I need a cup (from, of) sugar for this recipe.

_____

9. Is that guy (from, of) Mexico?

_____

10. I work (from, of) Monday to Thursday. I don't work Friday.

_____

11. Do you want a glass (from, of) beer?

_____

12. She is a woman (from, of) value in our company.

_____

13. The cat jumped (from, of) the couch to the window.

_____

14. Open the gift (from, of) me.

_____

EXERCISE
36·2

Use your dictionary to find the meaning of the new vocabulary words needed for this exercise before you begin. Write the words in your language in the space provided.

_____ monthly	_____ decade	_____ odor
_____ mouthful	_____ spoonful	_____ century
_____ herd	_____ popcorn	_____ theater
_____ seventy	_____ litter	_____ catalog

*Complete the following sentences with **from** or **of**.*

1. She brought a basket _____ fruit for us.

2. He is a man _____ experience.

3. We receive checks monthly _____ the insurance company.

4. The little girl has a mouthful _____ milk.

5. Are you _____ Montreal?

6. Put this box _____ books in the basement.

7. Do you want a cup _____ tea?

8. The odor is coming _____ the fridge.

9. I have a picture _____ you.

10. Take out a sheet _____ paper _____ your binder.

11. Do you want to play a game _____ cards?

12. My cat had a litter _____ kittens last night.

13. We get vitamins _____ food.

14. I bought a bag _____ popcorn at the theater.

15. She counted _____ one to seventy in French.

16. I borrowed it _____ my cousin.

17. What is the special _____ the day?

18. My uncle died _____ cancer.

19. I have a closet full _____ old shoes.

20. I just got home _____ school.

21. Who is the woman _____ the decade?

22. She moved _____ her apartment to a retirement home.

23. We just came back _____ Italy.

24. She works _____ her home office.

25. I ate a bowl _____ chicken soup for lunch.

26. We got a call _____ your teacher.

27. I need a spoonful _____ honey.

28. You have a message _____ Tom.

29. We picked fresh tomatoes _____ our garden.

30. Thank you for the box _____ chocolates.

31. There is a herd _____ horses in the field.

32. The gorilla escaped _____ the zoo.

33. Where is the jar _____ pickles?

34. I received a long e-mail _____ my aunt.

35. We drank a bottle _____ wine with dinner.

36. She ordered it _____ the new catalog.

37. Who is the person _____ the century?

38. I got the results _____ my doctor.

Will: Future Tense

Use **will** to create the future tense for all persons. The simple form of the verb always follows **will**.

I will	→	I will hold	→	I will hold your books.
you will	→	you will hold	→	You will hold the baby.
he will	→	he will hold	→	He will hold my hand.
she will	→	she will hold	→	She will hold her doll.
it will	→	it will hold	→	It will hold the ball.
we will	→	we will hold	→	We will hold our fishing rods.
they will	→	they will hold	→	They will hold the ladder.

EXERCISE

37·1

Use your dictionary to find the meaning of the following verbs and vocabulary words needed for this exercise before you begin. Write the words in your language in the space provided.

_____ to flip	_____ to reduce	_____ to envy
_____ to ship	_____ to enlarge	_____ to gather
_____ to hug	_____ to become	_____ to grant
_____ to ban	_____ to pamper	
_____ to introduce		

_____ fairy	_____ author	_____ raspberry
_____ top	_____ famous	_____ lighthouse
_____ tax	_____ cherry	_____ tobacco
_____ brain	_____ several	_____ swordfish
_____ rich	_____ blueberry	_____ friendship
_____ government		

Rewrite the following sentences in the future tense by using **will** *and the simple form of the verb in parentheses.*

1. I (to climb) to the top of the lighthouse to see the ships.

   _____

2. You (to become) a rich and famous author.

   _____

3. The government (to reduce) taxes next year.

   _____

4. The fairy (to grant) you several wishes.

   _____

5. My mother (to make) a cherry pie.

   _____

6. We (to study) the brain in my science class.

   _____

7. They (to enlarge) the picture of the swordfish that they caught.

   _____

8. We (to gather) blueberries, strawberries, and raspberries to make jam.

   _____

9. He (to hug) and kiss you when he sees you.

   _____

10. Brad (to introduce) me to his parents tomorrow night.

    _____

11. We (to ship) the package to you this afternoon.

    _____

12. Mary (to envy) your friendship with Paul.

    _____

13. The government (to ban) tobacco in all public places.

    _____

14. She (to pamper) her new baby.

    _____

15. I (to flip) the pancakes now.

    _____

Use your dictionary to find the meaning of the following verbs and vocabulary words needed for this exercise before you begin. Write the words in your language in the space provided.

to donate	to develop	to miss
to inform	to stimulate	to continue
to tame	to postpone	to calculate
to wonder	to nod	to balance
to cause	to last	to bake
to concentrate		

budget	muscle	fine (n)
bake sale	career	circus
music	pay	only
organ	drum	twice
speeding	once	lion
taste bud	outcome	why
wonderful	public transportation	

*Complete the sentences using **will** and the simple form of the verb in parentheses to create the future tense.*

1. Brian _____ (to calculate) his pay.
2. We _____ (to balance) our budget.
3. Denis _____ (to develop) his muscles at the gym.
4. They _____ (to concentrate) on their careers.
5. It _____ (to last) a long time.
6. We _____ (to postpone) the meeting.
7. He _____ (to learn) to play the drums.
8. They _____ (to tame) the lions for the circus.
9. I _____ (to tell) you only once.
10. They _____ (to wonder) why we left.
11. We _____ (to order) a pizza for supper.
12. The neighbors _____ (to move) next month.
13. I _____ (to miss) you.
14. She _____ (to bake) cookies for the bake sale.
15. Ricky Martin _____ (to continue) to make wonderful music.

16. It _____ (to be) cold tomorrow.

17. He _____ (to nod) his head twice.

18. We _____ (to use) public transportation.

19. You _____ (to get) a fine for speeding.

20. It _____ (to stimulate) your taste buds.

21. You _____ (to cause) a serious accident.

22. She _____ (to donate) her organs.

23. He _____ (to inform) us of the outcome.

24. Jim and Scott _____ (to share) the expenses.

Will: Future Tense: Negative Form

38

Place **not** after **will** to create the negative form of the future tense. The simple form of the verb always follows **will not**.

I will	→	I will not	→	I will not be there.
you will	→	you will not	→	You will not say that.
he will	→	he will not	→	He will not pay me.
she will	→	she will not	→	She will not see you.
it will	→	it will not	→	It will not eat.
we will	→	we will not	→	We will not borrow money.
they will	→	they will not	→	They will not drive to New York.

The negative form of the future tense with **will** can be expressed with the contraction **won't**.

I will not	→	I won't	→	I won't go.
you will not	→	you won't	→	You won't convince her.
he will not	→	he won't	→	He won't know.
she will not	→	she won't	→	She won't sleep late.
it will not	→	it won't	→	It won't bite you.
we will not	→	we won't	→	We won't spend a lot.
they will not	→	they won't	→	They won't help us.

EXERCISE
38·1

Use your dictionary to find the meaning of the following verbs and vocabulary words needed for this exercise before you begin. Write the words in your language in the space provided.

_____ to recognize	_____ to allow	_____ to trim
_____ to celebrate	_____ to pawn	_____ to stay
_____ to confess	_____ to declare	
_____ sideburns	_____ overnight	_____ guitar
_____ blind date	_____ murder	_____ bush
_____ bankruptcy	_____ New Year's Eve	

Rewrite the following sentences to create the negative form of the future tense. Write your answer once with **will not** *and once with the contraction* **won't**.

1. He will declare bankruptcy. _____

   _____

2. My neighbor will trim his bushes. _____

   _____

3. John will trim his sideburns. _____

   _____

4. Anna will go on a blind date. _____

   _____

5. You will recognize me with my wig. _____

   _____

6. They will allow you to stay overnight. _____

   _____

7. We will celebrate on New Year's Eve. _____

   _____

8. The man will confess to the murder. _____

   _____

9. I will pawn my guitar. _____

   _____

EXERCISE
38·2

Use your dictionary to find the meaning of the following verbs and vocabulary words needed for this exercise before you begin. Write the words in your language in the space provided.

_____ to delay   _____ to operate   _____ to clog

_____ to betray   _____ to issue   _____ to improve

_____ to hand   _____ to benefit   _____ to attempt

_____ to tolerate   _____ to guess   _____ to ruin

_____ to pierce   _____ to purchase   _____ to cure

_____ to compensate

_____ tool   _____ drain   _____ newsletter

_____ soap   _____ guilty   _____ will (n)

Will: Future Tense: Negative Form **127**

_____ job	_____ weight	_____ product
_____ flight	_____ hell	_____ wisdom teeth
_____ heaven	_____ spine	_____ loss
_____ breast	_____ custody	_____ reputation
_____ suit	_____ rundown	_____ insurance policy
_____ tongue	_____ jet	_____ agreement

Complete the following sentences by using the contraction **won't** *and the simple form of the verb in parentheses.*

1. You _____ (to ruin) your reputation.

2. It _____ (to clog) the drain.

3. My company _____ (to issue) the newsletter.

4. We _____ (to improve) our products this year.

5. I _____ (to guess) your weight.

6. They _____ (to discuss) heaven and hell.

7. We _____ (to benefit) from this insurance policy.

8. It _____ (to delay) our flight.

9. They _____ (to compensate) us for our loss.

10. She _____ (to allow) me to pierce my tongue.

11. The treatment _____ (to cure) breast cancer.

12. He _____ (to purchase) new tools for his job.

13. The students _____ (to listen) to their teacher.

14. The pilot _____ (to attempt) to fly the jet.

15. He _____ (to wear) his black suit.

16. They _____ (to sign) the agreement.

17. My aunt _____ (to make) a will.

18. The doctors _____ (to operate) on my spine.

19. We _____ (to betray) you.

20. My dentist _____ (to remove) my wisdom teeth.

21. She _____ (to have) custody of the children.

22. They _____ (to live) in a rundown building.

23. It _____ (to mean) that he is guilty.

24. I _____ (to tolerate) this behavior.

25. Louise _____ (to hand) me the soap.

26. You _____ (to fail) your exam.

Will: Future Tense: Question Form

Place **will** before the subject to create questions in the future tense. The simple form of the verb is always used when forming questions with **will**.

I will	→	will I like	→	Will I like it?
you will	→	will you call	→	Will you call me?
he will	→	will he write	→	Will he write a book?
she will	→	will she join	→	Will she join us for dinner?
it will	→	will it annoy	→	Will it annoy you?
we will	→	will we need	→	Will we need a new car?
they will	→	will they worry	→	Will they worry about me?

EXERCISE

39·1

Use your dictionary to find the meaning of the following verbs and vocabulary words needed for this exercise before you begin. Write the words in your language in the space provided.

_____ to travel   _____ to punish

_____ to spray   _____ to disappear

_____ to rescue   _____ to mention

_____ to kick   _____ to partake

_____ to accuse   _____ to show

_____ to poison   _____ to measure

_____ fang   _____ island   _____ brand-new

_____ wasp   _____ pajamas   _____ foreman

_____ bee   _____ writing   _____ competition

_____ muscle   _____ eagle   _____ last name

_____ toaster   _____ ironing board

_____ poison   _____ tape measure

*Rewrite the following sentences to create the question form of the future tense by placing **will** before the subject. Don't forget to include a question mark (?) in your answer.*

1. The snow will disappear in the spring.

   _____

2. Your mother will punish you for that.

   _____

3. The police will accuse Sara.

   _____

4. You will spell your last name for me.

   _____

5. She will throw her old pajamas in the garbage.

   _____

6. He will measure it with his brand-new tape measure.

   _____

7. Bobby will show the judges his muscles.

   _____

8. It will poison you with its fangs.

   _____

9. They will mention it to their foreman.

   _____

10. The gardener will spray the wasps and bees with poison.

    _____

11. They will rescue the eagles on the island.

    _____

12. Your boyfriend will partake in the writing competition.

    _____

13. We will travel a lot next year.

    _____

14. It will kick me.

    _____

15. She will buy a new ironing board and toaster for her apartment.

    _____

Use your dictionary to find the meaning of the following verbs and vocabulary words needed for this exercise before you begin. Write the words in your language in the space provided.

_____	to grind	_____	to publish	_____	to blame
_____	to produce	_____	to require	_____	to trade
_____	to sag	_____	to regret	_____	to expand
_____	to respond	_____	to pause	_____	to arrive

_____	stitch	_____	magnet	_____	ivory
_____	rush hour	_____	painting	_____	trailer
_____	mouth	_____	on time		

*Rewrite the following sentences to create questions in the future tense by placing **will** before the subject. Don't forget to include a question mark (?) in your answer.*

1. It will arrive on time. _____

2. He will publish his report. _____

3. They will blame me. _____

4. We will be in rush hour traffic. _____

5. Our country will ban the sale of ivory. _____

6. Sheila will stick the magnet on the fridge. _____

7. You will close your mouth when you eat. _____

8. We will produce a lot of corn this year. _____

9. Our company will expand next year. _____

10. It will rain tomorrow. _____

11. We will trade our trailer for a boat. _____

12. He will pause the movie for a few minutes. _____

13. I will regret it. _____

14. It will grind the coffee beans. _____

15. You will require stitches in your knee. _____

16. The roof will sag with all the snow on it. _____

17. They will bid on the famous painting. _____

18. I will gain weight if I eat this. _____

19. He will respond. _____

20. I will have enough time. _____

40· *Be Going To*: Future Tense

The future tense can also be expressed by using **be going to**. Use the correct form of the verb **to be** for each person. The simple form of the verb always follows **be going to**.

I am going to	→	I am going to explain	→	I am going to explain it to you again.
you are going to	→	you are going to need	→	You are going to need a hammer.
he is going to	→	he is going to answer	→	He is going to answer the question.
she is going to	→	she is going to have	→	She is going to have a baby.
it is going to	→	it is going to be	→	It is going to be expensive.
we are going to	→	we are going to prove	→	We are going to prove it to you.
they are going to	→	they are going to meet	→	They are going to meet downtown.

EXERCISE
40·1

Use your dictionary to find the meaning of the following verbs and vocabulary words needed for this exercise before you begin. Write the words in your language in the space provided.

_____ to lift	_____ to spread	_____ to hurry
_____ to dirty	_____ to injure	_____ to applaud
_____ to shine	_____ to vomit	_____ to remove
_____ to check	_____ to create	_____ to surprise
_____ sun	_____ lobby	_____ shallow
_____ end	_____ schedule	_____ muddy
_____ deep	_____ too much	_____ audience
_____ upset	_____ manager	_____ waterbed

Rewrite the following sentences in the future tense using **be going to**. *Use the correct form of the verb* **to be** *and the simple form of the verb in parentheses.*

1. I (be) going to (to hurry) because I don't want to miss my bus.

   _____

2. He drank too much, and now he (be) going to (to vomit).

   _____

3. You (be) going to (to dirty) my floor with your muddy shoes.

   _____

4. The sun (be) going to (to shine) all day today.

   _____

5. I (be) going to (to wait) for you in the lobby downstairs.

   _____

6. We (be) going to (to sell) our waterbed in our garage sale.

   _____

7. The kids (be) going to (to swim) in the shallow end of the pool.

   _____

8. The adults (be) going to (to dive) in the deep end of the pool.

   _____

9. You (be) going to (to injure) your back if you lift that heavy box.

   _____

10. It (be) going to (to create) problems in the office.

   _____

11. I (be) going to (to spread) the jam on my toast.

   _____

12. My manager (be) going to (to check) his schedule for next week.

   _____

13. You (be) going to (to be) upset if the audience doesn't applaud.

   _____

14. He (be) going to (to surprise) her with a diamond ring.

   _____

15. She (be) going to (to remove) your name from the list.

   _____

Use your dictionary to find the meaning of the following verbs and vocabulary words needed for this exercise before you begin. Write the words in your language in the space provided.

_____ to tighten	_____ to commute	_____ to tap
_____ to assume	_____ to admit	_____ to seem
_____ to skip	_____ to suggest	_____ to vanish
_____ to remind	_____ to clip	_____ to charge
_____ sample	_____ hairspray	_____ noon
_____ dawn	_____ someday	_____ proud
_____ partner	_____ interest	_____ difficult
_____ receipt	_____ turnip	_____ at first
_____ painful	_____ shallot	_____ leash
_____ innocent		

*Complete the sentences using the correct form of the verb **to be** and the simple form of the verb in parentheses to create the future tense with **be going to**.*

1. We _____ going to _____ (to assume) that he is innocent.

2. He _____ going to _____ (to suggest) something better at the meeting.

3. She _____ going to _____ (to tighten) the leash on the dog.

4. I _____ going to _____ (to clip) the receipts together.

5. We _____ going to _____ (to observe) the students in the cafeteria at noon.

6. I _____ going to _____ (to give) you a sample.

7. It _____ going to _____ (to seem) difficult at first.

8. We _____ going to _____ (to remind) you in the morning.

9. We _____ going to _____ (to admit) the truth.

10. It _____ going to _____ (to be) very painful.

11. He _____ going to _____ (to ask) his partner.

12. I _____ going to _____ (to tap) him on the shoulder.

13. The students _____ going to _____ (to commute) by train.

14. The boys _____ going to _____ (to skip) school this afternoon.

15. I _____ going to _____ (to put) shallots and turnips in the stew.

16. She _____ going to _____ (to marry) Edward someday.

17. It _____ going to _____ (to occur) at dawn.

18. They _____ going to _____ (to charge) us interest.

19. This car _____ going to _____ (to belong) to me someday.

20. The fog _____ going to _____ (to vanish) soon.

21. I _____ going to _____ (to buy) a can of hairspray.

22. You _____ going to _____ (to be) very proud.

Be Going To: Future Tense: Negative Form

Place **not** after the verb **to be** to create the negative form of the future tense with **be going to**. The simple form of the verb always follows the negative form of **be going to**.

I am going to	→	I am not going to	→	I am not going to lose.
you are going to	→	you are not going to	→	You are not going to win.
he is going to	→	he is not going to	→	He is not going to be there.
she is going to	→	she is not going to	→	She is not going to eat it.
it is going to	→	it is not going to	→	It is not going to run.
we are going to	→	we are not going to	→	We are not going to leave.
they are going to	→	they are not going to	→	They are not going to talk.

The negative form of the future tense with **be going to** can also be expressed with the contraction **isn't** or **aren't**. There is no contraction for **am not**.

I am not going to	→		→	I am not going to drive.
you are not going to	→	you aren't going to	→	You aren't going to forget.
he is not going to	→	he isn't going to	→	He isn't going to play.
she is not going to	→	she isn't going to	→	She isn't going to study.
it is not going to	→	it isn't going to	→	It isn't going to rain.
we are not going to	→	we aren't going to	→	We aren't going to try it.
they are not going to	→	they aren't going to	→	They aren't going to like it.

EXERCISE

41·1

Use your dictionary to find the meaning of the following verbs and vocabulary words needed for this exercise before you begin. Write the words in your language in the space provided.

_____ to haunt   _____ to submit   _____ to reuse

_____ to chill   _____ to invest   _____ to divorce

_____ to withdraw   _____ to announce

_____ funds   _____ report   _____ stock market

_____ life   _____ ostrich   _____ experience

_____ rest   _____ cutbacks

Rewrite the following sentences to create the negative form of the future tense of **be going to**. *Write your answer once with* **am not, is not,** *or* **are not** *and once with the contraction* **isn't** *or* **aren't**.

1. My company is going to announce cutbacks for the new year. _____

_____

2. We are going to submit the report in the morning. _____

_____

3. I am going to withdraw all my money. _____

_____

4. They are going to invest the funds in the stock market. _____

_____

5. This experience is going to haunt me for the rest of my life. _____

_____

6. Annie is going to chill the wine before she serves it. _____

_____

7. The ostrich is going to attack you. _____

_____

8. You are going to reuse the bags. _____

_____

9. He is going to divorce his wife. _____

_____

EXERCISE
41·2

Use your dictionary to find the meaning of the following verbs and vocabulary words needed for this exercise before you begin. Write the words in your language in the space provided.

_____ to judge   _____ to wrestle   _____ to trap

_____ to steer   _____ to quarrel   _____ to label

_____ to pry   _____ to trick   _____ to respect

_____ to curse   _____ to care   _____ to ensure

_____ to lessen   _____ to leap   _____ to can

_____ to empty

_____ checkers   _____ safety   _____ pain

_____ subpoena   _____ January   _____ February

_____ March   _____ April   _____ May

_____ June   _____ beet   _____ bailiff

*Complete the following sentences using **am not** or the contraction **isn't** or **aren't** to create the negative form of the future tense of **be going to**.*

1. We _____ going to trick you again.

2. She _____ going to circle the right answer.

3. We _____ going to respect his decision.

4. They _____ going to ensure our safety.

5. You _____ going to curse in my class.

6. She _____ going to empty her purse.

7. I _____ going to label all the items in the store.

8. We _____ going to can beets this year.

9. She _____ going to care about that.

10. We _____ going to send the subpoena by bailiff.

11. It _____ going to snow in June.

12. I _____ going to be twenty-five years old in January.

13. She _____ going to visit me in March.

14. You _____ going to have another operation.

15. They _____ going to play checkers all night.

16. I _____ going to bake a cake.

17. Nancy _____ going to place the names in a hat.

18. We _____ going to judge you.

19. It _____ going to lessen the pain.

20. The frog _____ going to leap on you.

21. They _____ going to quarrel again.

22. He _____ going to pry the door open.

23. Sidney _____ going to steer the boat.

24. The boys _____ going to wrestle in the living room.

25. We _____ going to be in Tokyo in April.

26. He _____ going to start his new job in May.

27. It _____ going to open in February.

28. We _____ going to trap beavers.

Be Going To: Future Tense: Question Form

·42·

Place the verb **to be** before the subject to create questions in the future tense of **be going to**. The simple form of the verb is always used when forming questions with **be going to**.

I am going to	→	am I going to	→	Am I going to see you?
you are going to	→	are you going to	→	Are you going to visit me?
he is going to	→	is he going to	→	Is he going to believe you?
she is going to	→	is she going to	→	Is she going to be here?
it is going to	→	is it going to	→	Is it going to start soon?
we are going to	→	are we going to	→	Are we going to agree?
they are going to	→	are they going to	→	Are they going to park there?

EXERCISE
42·1

Use your dictionary to find the meaning of the following verbs and vocabulary words needed for this exercise before you begin. Write the words in your language in the space provided.

	to dip		to store		to process
	to graze		to apply		to supply
	to turn		to scrub		to provide
	to drain		to immigrate		
	to cooperate				

	July		September
	parents		United States
	bathtub		November
	peace		December
	supplies		explanation
	August		knowledge
	war		immigration
	October		snowblower

Rewrite the following sentences to create the question form of the future tense of **be going to** *by placing the verb* **to be** *before the subject. Don't forget to include a question mark (?) in your answer.*

1. He is going to share this knowledge with the world.

   _____

2. She is going to cooperate with us.

   _____

3. You are going to provide me with a good explanation.

   _____

4. They are going to immigrate to the United States in August.

   _____

5. It is going to turn green when I put it in water.

   _____

6. The immigration office is going to process my file in July.

   _____

7. My parents are going to supply me with my school supplies in September.

   _____

8. I am going to drain the vegetables with this.

   _____

9. They are going to complete the project in November or December.

   _____

10. She is going to apply for a new job in October.

    _____

11. You are going to scrub the bathtub now.

    _____

12. The cows and horses are going to graze in the field.

    _____

13. You are going to dip the apple in honey.

    _____

14. We are going to store the snowblower in the garage during the summer.

    _____

15. The teacher is going to talk about war and peace in history class today.

    _____

Use your dictionary to find the meaning of the following verbs and vocabulary words needed for this exercise before you begin. Write the words in your language in the space provided.

_____ to compete   _____ to tidy   _____ to wish

_____ to promise   _____ to assess   _____ to sort

_____ to rest   _____ to whistle

_____ second   _____ sunny   _____ shrimp

_____ werewolf   _____ customs   _____ interview

_____ icicle   _____ oven mitts

*Rewrite the following sentences to create questions in the future tense of **be going to** by placing the verb* **to be** *before the subject. Don't forget to include a question mark (?) in your answer.*

1. He is going to promise to be good.

   _____

2. You are going to wish for a car again.

   _____

3. I am going to compete with you.

   _____

4. She is going to rest on the couch.

   _____

5. You are going to fake that you are sick.

   _____

6. He is going to break the icicles with the shovel.

   _____

7. Sonia is going to buy new oven mitts.

   _____

8. The insurance company is going to assess the damage.

   _____

9. You are going to cry.

   _____

10. It is going to be sunny tomorrow.

    _____

11. I am going to have a second interview.

_____

12. We are going to wait a long time at customs.

_____

13. She is going to sort the dirty laundry.

_____

14. Bobby is going to tidy his room.

_____

15. We are going to watch the scary movie about the werewolf.

_____

16. They are going to whistle the song.

_____

17. They are going to bring shrimp to the party tomorrow night.

_____

18. It is going to be good.

_____

The Indefinite Articles: A and An

The indefinite articles **a** and **an** are used with singular nouns. Use **a** before most nouns or adjectives that begin with a consonant. Use **an** before most nouns or adjectives that begin with a vowel.

a cup	a ball	a class	a bug
an empty cup	an orange ball	an English class	an ugly bug
an egg	an idea	an owl	an accident
a brown egg	a good idea	a white owl	a bad accident

Use **a** before nouns or adjectives that begin with a pronounced **h**, but use **an** before nouns or adjectives when the **h** is not pronounced.

a house	a horse	a hammer	a hurricane
an honor	an hour	an heir	an honest mistake

Use **a** before nouns or adjectives if the vowel is pronounced as a consonant. The following words are pronounced with a **y** sound.

a union	a university	a uniform	a utensil

The following words are pronounced with a **w** sound.

a one-hour class	a once-in-a-lifetime opportunity

EXERCISE
43·1

*Rewrite the following sentences correctly by choosing **a** or **an**.*

1. We saw (a, an) horrible accident this morning. _____

   _____

2. This is (a, an) one-way street. _____

3. My uncle has (a, an) ostrich on his farm. _____

   _____

4. He is (a, an) American citizen. _____

5. I wear (a, an) uniform to work. _____

143

6. There was (a, an) earthquake last night. _____

_____

7. You are (a, an) excellent student. _____

8. I need (a, an) hammer to fix the roof. _____

9. It was (a, an) useful tool. _____

10. I have (a, an) red apple in my lunch bag. _____

11. We bought (a, an) oil painting at the market. _____

_____

12. This is (a, an) busy airport. _____

13. Give me (a, an) example, please. _____

14. We played the game for (a, an) hour and (a, an) half. _____

_____

Complete the following sentences with **a** *or* **an**.

1. I ate _____ orange, _____ banana, and _____ peach today.

2. There is _____ wild ostrich in the field.

3. I want to live on _____ island for _____ month.

4. Give her _____ application, please.

5. There is _____ spider, _____ ant, and _____ fly in the kitchen.

6. You made _____ excellent effort.

7. Do you want _____ oatmeal cookie?

8. We have _____ union at work.

9. Do you have _____ horse?

10. I had _____ egg sandwich for lunch.

11. She married _____ wealthy American.

12. We made _____ apple cake, _____ salad, and _____ onion dip for the picnic.

13. Do you have _____ yellow umbrella?

14. I saw _____ owl, _____ tiger, _____ eagle, _____ zebra, and _____ elephant at the zoo.

15. She has _____ blue eye and _____ green eye.

16. Do you have _____ appointment?

17. She is _____ heir to the estate.

18. I have _____ idea.

19. He drew _____ picture of _____ unicorn.

20. We had _____ ice storm and _____ hurricane last year.

21. I prefer to wear _____ one-piece bathing suit to the beach.

22. It is _____ honor to meet you.

23. Is there _____ university in your city?

24. That is _____ honest opinion.

25. I want _____ ice cube and _____ cherry in my drink.

26. We had _____ easy test at school.

27. I need _____ cup of olive oil.

28. There is _____ oil lamp in the living room.

29. We saw _____ dead octopus on the beach.

30. I found _____ old sock under the bed.

31. It was _____ expensive ring.

32. There is _____ pen, _____ pencil, and _____ eraser on the table.

33. You are _____ hero.

34. You need _____ envelope and _____ stamp if you want to send _____ letter.

35. My sister had _____ baby; now I am _____ aunt.

36. Is there _____ elevator in the building?

37. It has _____ long nose.

38. We have _____ uncle in Germany.

39. I want _____ second opinion.

40. Do you want _____ ice-cream cone?

Irregular Verbs Table

Study and learn the past participles of the following irregular verbs.

SIMPLE FORM	SIMPLE PAST	PAST PARTICIPLE
awake	awoke	awoken
be	was/were	been
beat	beat	beaten
become	became	become
begin	began	begun
bend	bent	bent
bet	bet	bet
bite	bit	bitten
bleed	bled	bled
blow	blew	blown
break	broke	broken
bring	brought	brought
broadcast	broadcast	broadcast
build	built	built
burn	burned/burnt	burned/burnt
burst	burst	burst
buy	bought	bought
cast	cast	cast
catch	caught	caught
choose	chose	chosen
come	came	come
cost	cost	cost
creep	crept	crept
cut	cut	cut
deal	dealt	dealt
dig	dug	dug
dive	dived/dove	dived/dove
do	did	done
draw	drew	drawn
dream	dreamed/dreamt	dreamed/dreamt
drink	drank	drunk
drive	drove	driven
eat	ate	eaten
fall	fell	fallen
feed	fed	fed

SIMPLE FORM	SIMPLE PAST	PAST PARTICIPLE
feel	felt	felt
fight	fought	fought
find	found	found
fit	fit	fit
flee	fled	fled
fly	flew	flown
forbid	forbade	forbidden
forget	forgot	forgotten
forgive	forgave	forgiven
freeze	froze	frozen
get	got	got/gotten
give	gave	given
go	went	gone
grind	ground	ground
grow	grew	grown
hang	hung	hung
have	had	had
hear	heard	heard
hide	hid	hidden
hit	hit	hit
hold	held	held
hurt	hurt	hurt
keep	kept	kept
kneel	knelt	knelt
knit	knitted/knit	knitted/knit
know	knew	known
lay (to place, put down)	laid	laid
lead	led	led
leave	left	left
lend	lent	lent
let	let	let
lie (to lie down)	lay	lain
light	lit	lit
lose	lost	lost
make	made	made
mean	meant	meant
meet	met	met
mistake	mistook	mistaken
pay	paid	paid
prove	proved	proved/proven
put	put	put
quit	quit	quit
read	read	read
ride	rode	ridden
ring	rang	rung
rise	rose	risen
run	ran	run
say	said	said
see	saw	seen
seek	sought	sought

SIMPLE FORM	SIMPLE PAST	PAST PARTICIPLE
sell	sold	sold
send	sent	sent
set	set	set
sew	sewed	sewed/sewn
shake	shook	shaken
shave	shaved	shaved/shaven
shear	sheared	sheared/shorn
shed	shed	shed
shine	shined/shone	shined/shone
shoot	shot	shot
show	showed	shown
shrink	shrank	shrunk
shut	shut	shut
sing	sang	sung
sink	sank	sunk
sit	sat	sat
sleep	slept	slept
slide	slid	slid
speak	spoke	spoken
spend	spent	spent
spill	spilled/spilt	spilled/spilt
spin	spun	spun
spit	spit/spat	spit/spat
split	split	split
spread	spread	spread
spring	sprang	sprung
stand	stood	stood
steal	stole	stolen
stick	stuck	stuck
sting	stung	stung
strike	struck	struck
swear	swore	sworn
sweep	swept	swept
swell	swelled	swelled/swollen
swim	swam	swum
swing	swung	swung
take	took	taken
teach	taught	taught
tear	tore	torn
tell	told	told
think	thought	thought
throw	threw	thrown
understand	understood	understood
upset	upset	upset
wake	woke	woken
wear	wore	worn
weep	wept	wept
win	won	won
write	wrote	written

The Present Perfect Tense

The present perfect tense is used when the time of a past activity is not important or is not known in the sentence. Use **has** or **have** and the past participle of the verb with both regular and irregular verbs to form the present perfect tense.

Contractions can also be used with the pronouns to create the present perfect tense.

Regular

SIMPLE PRESENT	SIMPLE PAST	PRESENT PERFECT	CONTRACTION
I work	I worked	I have worked	I've worked
you work	you worked	you have worked	you've worked
he works	he worked	he has worked	he's worked
she works	she worked	she has worked	she's worked
it works	it worked	it has worked	it's worked
we work	we worked	we have worked	we've worked
they work	they worked	they have worked	they've worked

Irregular

SIMPLE PRESENT	SIMPLE PAST	PRESENT PERFECT	CONTRACTION
I take	I took	I have taken	I've taken
you take	you took	you have taken	you've taken
he takes	he took	he has taken	he's taken
she takes	she took	she has taken	she's taken
it takes	it took	it has taken	it's taken
we take	we took	we have taken	we've taken
they take	they took	they have taken	they've taken

The past participle of all regular verbs is the same as the simple past tense form (add **-ed**).

INFINITIVE	SIMPLE PAST	PAST PARTICIPLE
to borrow	borrowed	borrowed
to cheat	cheated	cheated
to try	tried	tried
to offend	offended	offended
to work	worked	worked

The past participle of all irregular verbs has a different form and must be studied and learned. Refer to Lesson 44.

INFINITIVE	SIMPLE PAST	PAST PARTICIPLE
to grow	grew	grown
to teach	taught	taught
to be	was/were	been
to hear	heard	heard
to take	took	taken

It takes a lot of practice to be able to correctly use the present perfect tense. Learn the past participles of all the irregular verbs by heart, and you will quickly be able to use this tense proficiently.

EXERCISE 45·1

*Rewrite the following sentences to create the present perfect tense using **has** or **have** and the past participle of the verb in parentheses. Use the two preceding verb lists to complete this exercise. You have already learned these verbs in previous exercises.*

1. They (to work) in Japan.

   _____

2. William (to grow) a lot since the last time I saw him.

   _____

3. My parents (to be) together for twenty years.

   _____

4. They (to borrow) a lot of money from their friends.

   _____

5. She (to teach) English in many different schools.

   _____

6. You (to offend) everybody in the office.

   _____

7. I (to hear) that noise in my car several times.

   _____

8. He (to cheat) on every one of his tests.

   _____

9. We (to try) to help them.

   _____

10. It (to take) a long time.

   _____

Complete the sentences that follow to create the present perfect tense. Use the contracted pronoun and the past participle of the verb in parentheses. You have already learned these verbs in previous exercises.

Regular

INFINITIVE	SIMPLE PAST	PAST PARTICIPLE
to offer	offered	offered
to climb	climbed	climbed
to use	used	used
to discuss	discussed	discussed
to warn	warned	warned
to accuse	accused	accused
to suffer	suffered	suffered
to help	helped	helped
to start	started	started
to thank	thanked	thanked

Irregular

INFINITIVE	SIMPLE PAST	PAST PARTICIPLE
to forgive	forgave	forgiven
to bite	bit	bitten
to make	made	made
to sing	sang	sung
to see	saw	seen
to tear	tore	torn
to choose	chose	chosen
to know	knew	known
to break	broke	broken
to fly	flew	flown

1. He _____ (to break) the law many times.

2. I _____ (to use) this product before.

3. We _____ (to see) that movie several times.

4. He _____ (to make) many mistakes in his life.

5. It _____ (to bite) a few people.

6. You _____ (to offer) to help.

7. I _____ (to fly) many times.

8. They _____ (to suffer) enough.

9. You _____ (to tear) all the clothes I lent you.

10. She _____ (to forgive) you many times.

11. I _____ (to know) Mary since high school.

12. He _____ (to accuse) me of that before.

13. It _____ (to start).

14. We _____ (to discuss) this many times.

15. I _____ (to warn) you about that.

16. It _____ (to help) me to be a better person.

17. We _____ (to choose) to live in the city.

18. She _____ (to sing) that song before.

19. They _____ (to thank) us ten times.

20. He _____ (to climb) many mountains.

The Present Perfect Tense: Negative Form

Place **not** after **has** or **have** to create the negative form of the present perfect tense. Use the past participle of the verb in the negative form.

I have been	→	I have not been	→	I have not been to Paris.
you have been	→	you have not been	→	You have not been there.
he has been	→	he has not been	→	He has not been nice.
she has been	→	she has not been	→	She has not been happy.
it has been	→	it has not been	→	It has not been cold.
we have been	→	we have not been	→	We have not been busy.
they have been	→	they have not been	→	They have not been on a boat.

The negative form of the present perfect tense can also be expressed with the contraction **hasn't** or **haven't**.

I have not seen	→	I haven't seen	→	I haven't seen it.
you have not seen	→	you haven't seen	→	You haven't seen the play.
he has not seen	→	he hasn't seen	→	He hasn't seen his sister.
she has not seen	→	she hasn't seen	→	She hasn't seen her brother.
it has not seen	→	it hasn't seen	→	It hasn't seen me.
we have not seen	→	we haven't seen	→	We haven't seen the movie.
they have not seen	→	they haven't seen	→	They haven't seen Sara.

The past participle of all regular verbs is the same as the simple past tense form (add **-ed**).

INFINITIVE	SIMPLE PAST	PAST PARTICIPLE
to attract	attracted	attracted
to wait	waited	waited
to accept	accepted	accepted
to invent	invented	invented

The past participle of all irregular verbs has a different form and must be studied and learned. Refer to Lesson 44.

INFINITIVE	SIMPLE PAST	PAST PARTICIPLE
to find	found	found
to become	became	become
to write	wrote	written

Rewrite the following sentences to create the negative form of the present perfect tense.
*Write your answer once with **has not** or **have not** and once with the contraction **hasn't** or*
***haven't**. Use the past participle of the verb in parentheses. You have already learned these*
verbs in previous exercises.

1. My teacher (to write) two books. _____

   _____

2. I (to accept) the offer. _____

   _____

3. They (to invent) many fun games. _____

   _____

4. The light (to attract) all the bugs. _____

   _____

5. Joe and Lynn (to become) rich and famous. _____

   _____

6. We (to find) that he works very hard. _____

   _____

7. Cassandra (to wait) a long time for the news. _____

   _____

Use your dictionary to find the meaning of the new vocabulary words needed for this
exercise before you begin. Write the words in your language in the space provided.

_____ chore   _____ chance   _____ team

_____ prisoner   _____ feelings   _____ secret

_____ tattoo   _____ Italy

*Complete the sentences that follow by using the contraction **hasn't** or **haven't** and the past participle of*
the verb in parentheses. You have already learned these verbs in previous exercises.

Regular

INFINITIVE	SIMPLE PAST	PAST PARTICIPLE
to solve	solved	solved
to waste	wasted	wasted
to express	expressed	expressed
to convince	convinced	convinced

to notice	noticed	noticed
to escape	escaped	escaped
to ask	asked	asked

Irregular

INFINITIVE	SIMPLE PAST	PAST PARTICIPLE
to give	gave	given
to have	had	had
to keep	kept	kept
to build	built	built
to go	went	gone
to fall	fell	fallen
to beat	beat	beaten
to do	did	done
to forget	forgot	forgotten

1. We _____ _____ (to keep) it a secret.

2. She _____ _____ (to notice) your new tattoo.

3. They _____ _____ (to go) to Italy.

4. Laura _____ _____ (to convince) me.

5. Mr. Lawrence _____ _____ (to build) three houses.

6. I _____ _____ (to do) all my chores.

7. Cindy _____ _____ (to express) her feelings.

8. You _____ _____ (to waste) my time.

9. You _____ _____ (to give) it a chance.

10. I _____ _____ (to solve) the mystery.

11. Jarrod _____ _____ (to have) his vacation.

12. I _____ _____ (to ask) for a raise twice.

13. My team _____ _____ (to beat) their team.

14. The prisoners _____ _____ (to escape) from jail.

15. It _____ _____ (to fall) asleep.

16. She _____ _____ (to forget) that it's your birthday.

The Present Perfect Tense: Question Form

47

Place **has** or **have** before the subject to create questions with the present perfect tense. The past participle of the verb is used when forming questions with the present perfect tense.

I have begun	→	have I begun	→	Have I begun to sing better?
you have begun	→	have you begun	→	Have you begun your course?
he has begun	→	has he begun	→	Has he begun to realize it?
she has begun	→	has she begun	→	Has she begun to understand?
it has begun	→	has it begun	→	Has it begun to melt?
we have begun	→	have we begun	→	Have we begun to eat right?
they have begun	→	have they begun	→	Have they begun to worry?

The past participle of all regular verbs is the same as the simple past tense form (add **-ed**).

INFINITIVE	SIMPLE PAST	PAST PARTICIPLE
to apologize	apologized	apologized
to benefit	benefited	benefited
to chew	chewed	chewed
to follow	followed	followed
to correct	corrected	corrected
to wrap	wrapped	wrapped

The past participle of all irregular verbs has a different form and must be studied and learned. Refer to Lesson 44.

INFINITIVE	SIMPLE PAST	PAST PARTICIPLE
to rise	rose	risen
to hide	hid	hidden
to show	showed	shown
to bring	brought	brought
to awake	awoke	awoken
to pay	paid	paid
to draw	drew	drawn
to blow	blew	blown

*Rewrite the following sentences to create the question form of the present perfect tense by placing **has** or **have** before the subject. Use the past participle of the verb in parentheses. You have already learned these verbs in previous exercises. Don't forget to include a question mark (?) in your answer.*

1. You (to show) your report card to your parents. _____

2. The teacher (to correct) all the exams. _____

3. I (to bring) enough for everybody. _____

4. My dog (to chew) all the furniture. _____

5. It (to follow) me to school often. _____

6. We (to wrap) all the gifts. _____

7. She (to blow) out all the candles on the cake. _____

8. They (to apologize) many times. _____

9. He (to draw) many beautiful pictures for her. _____

10. We (to benefit) from that. _____

11. It (to hide) the peanuts. _____

12. I (to pay) all the bills. _____

13. The sun (to rise). _____

14. I (to awake) the baby again. _____

*Rewrite the sentences that follow to create questions in the present perfect tense. Place **has** or **have** before the subject, and use the past participle of the verb in parentheses. You have already learned these verbs in previous exercises. Don't forget to include a question mark (?) in your answer.*

Regular

INFINITIVE	SIMPLE PAST	PAST PARTICIPLE
to invest	invested	invested
to occur	occurred	occurred
to iron	ironed	ironed
to answer	answered	answered
to park	parked	parked
to disappear	disappeared	disappeared
to manage	managed	managed

Irregular

INFINITIVE	SIMPLE PAST	PAST PARTICIPLE
to leave	left	left
to read	read	read
to drive	drove	driven
to meet	met	met
to sleep	slept	slept
to lose	lost	lost
to feed	fed	fed

1. You (to iron) the clothes. _____

2. He (to drive) many miles. _____

3. Leora (to answer) all the questions. _____

4. They (to feed) the animals. _____

5. It (to occur) a few times. _____

6. I (to read) that book before. _____

7. We (to invest) all our money. _____

8. I (to park) here before. _____

9. You (to lose) a lot of weight. _____

10. He (to manage) the company alone. _____

11. Elvis (to leave) the building. _____

12. It (to disappear). _____

13. Robin (to meet) many famous people. _____

14. George (to sleep) late many times. _____

The Past Perfect Tense

48

The past perfect tense is used to describe a past action that occurred before another past action. For example, one past action occurred at 8:00 P.M., and the previous past action occurred at 7:00 P.M. Use **had** for all persons and the past participle of the verb to create the past perfect tense.

I have heard	→	I had heard	→	I had heard the news.
you have heard	→	you had heard	→	You had heard the guitar.
he has heard	→	he had heard	→	He had heard you scream.
she has heard	→	she had heard	→	She had heard the song.
it has heard	→	it had heard	→	It had heard the noise.
we have heard	→	we had heard	→	We had heard everything.
they have heard	→	they had heard	→	They had heard nothing.

The contraction **'d** is often used with the pronouns when using the past perfect tense.

I had learned	→	I'd learned	→	I'd learned my lesson.
you had learned	→	you'd learned	→	You'd learned how to do it.
he had learned	→	he'd learned	→	He'd learned the rules.
she had learned	→	she'd learned	→	She'd learned our names.
it had learned	→	it'd learned	→	It'd learned how to speak.
we had learned	→	we'd learned	→	We'd learned to add.
they had learned	→	they'd learned	→	They'd learned to spell.

The past participle of all regular verbs is the same as the simple past tense form (add **-ed**).

INFINITIVE	SIMPLE PAST	PAST PARTICIPLE
to stop	stopped	stopped
to expect	expected	expected
to pass	passed	passed
to explain	explained	explained
to die	died	died
to decide	decided	decided

The past participle of all irregular verbs has a different form and must be studied and learned. Refer to Lesson 44.

INFINITIVE	SIMPLE PAST	PAST PARTICIPLE
to sell	sold	sold
to see	saw	seen
to have	had	had
to do	did	done

*Rewrite the following sentences to create the past perfect tense. Use **had** and the past participle of the verb in parentheses. You have already learned these verbs in previous exercises.*

1. We (to decide) to stay home when they asked us to go out for dinner.

   _____

2. They (to sell) their boat when they bought the motorcycle.

   _____

3. He (to expect) to see you before you left.

   _____

4. I (to have) supper, so I only ate the dessert.

   _____

5. My grandmother (to die) when I was born.

   _____

6. The rain (to stop), so we went for a walk.

   _____

7. I (to do) the laundry when he brought me his dirty clothes.

   _____

8. She (to see) the movie before, so she went to bed.

   _____

9. The teacher (to explain) the lesson twice, but we didn't understand.

   _____

10. We (to pass) all our exams, so we celebrated all night.

    _____

*Complete the sentences that follow using **had** and the past participle of the verb in parentheses. You have already learned these verbs in previous exercises.*

Regular

INFINITIVE	SIMPLE PAST	PAST PARTICIPLE
to finish	finished	finished
to order	ordered	ordered
to divorce	divorced	divorced
to rescue	rescued	rescued

to open	opened	opened
to complete	completed	completed
to worry	worried	worried

Irregular

INFINITIVE	SIMPLE PAST	PAST PARTICIPLE
to sweep	swept	swept
to throw	threw	thrown
to ring	rang	rung
to run	ran	run
to ride	rode	ridden
to sing	sang	sung
to cut	cut	cut

1. She _____ (to throw) it in the garbage when you asked for it.

2. We _____ (to sing) the song several times, but we forgot the words.

3. I _____ (to open) the gift when I realized it was for you.

4. They _____ (to order) the pizza when we arrived.

5. I _____ (to sweep) the floor when he dropped the plate of cookies.

6. We _____ (to worry) all night; then he finally called.

7. She _____ (to ride) the horse many times before she fell and broke her leg.

8. I _____ (to run) five miles when they cancelled the race.

9. He _____ (to complete) his homework, so he went to bed.

10. The class _____ (to finish) when we arrived.

11. The bell _____ (to ring) for twenty minutes before the janitor came to fix it.

12. We _____ (to rescue) the little girl in the water when the police came.

13. I _____ (to cut) my hair when he told me that he liked it long.

14. They _____ (to divorce) but remained good friends.

49

The Past Perfect Tense: Negative Form

Place **not** after **had** to create the negative form of the past perfect tense. The past participle of the verb is always used in the negative form.

I had run	→	I had not run	→	I had not run after school.
you had run	→	you had not run	→	You had not run very far.
he had run	→	he had not run	→	He had not run the race.
she had run	→	she had not run	→	She had not run with shoes.
it had run	→	it had not run	→	It had not run across the road.
we had run	→	we had not run	→	We had not run together.
they had run	→	they had not run	→	They had not run outside.

The negative form of the past perfect tense can also be expressed with the contraction **hadn't**.

I had not opened	→	I hadn't opened	→	I hadn't opened the mail.
you had not opened	→	you hadn't opened	→	You hadn't opened the book.
he had not opened	→	he hadn't opened	→	He hadn't opened the letter.
she had not opened	→	she hadn't opened	→	She hadn't opened her gifts.
it had not opened	→	it hadn't opened	→	It hadn't opened its mouth.
we had not opened	→	we hadn't opened	→	We hadn't opened the store.
they had not opened	→	they hadn't opened	→	They hadn't opened it.

The past participle of all regular verbs is the same as the simple past tense form (add **-ed**).

INFINITIVE	SIMPLE PAST	PAST PARTICIPLE
to notice	noticed	noticed
to follow	followed	followed
to arrive	arrived	arrived

The past participle of all irregular verbs has a different form and must be studied and learned. Refer to Lesson 44.

INFINITIVE	SIMPLE PAST	PAST PARTICIPLE
to fly	flew	flown
to pay	paid	paid
to see	saw	seen
to hold	held	held

*Rewrite the following sentences to create the negative form of the past perfect tense. Write your answer once with **had not** and once with the contraction **hadn't**. Use the past participle of the verb in parentheses. You have already learned these verbs in previous exercises.*

1. He (to hold) a baby before today. _____

   _____

2. It (to arrive), so I called the store. _____

   _____

3. I (to notice) that you were standing there. _____

   _____

4. She (to pay) the phone bill, so I paid it. _____

   _____

5. They (to see) that movie before, and they really enjoyed it. _____

   _____

6. We (to fly) before, so we were very nervous on the airplane. _____

   _____

7. You (to follow) the instructions, and you made a mistake. _____

   _____

*Complete the sentences that follow by using the contraction **hadn't** and the past participle of the verb in parentheses. You have already learned these verbs in previous exercises.*

Regular

INFINITIVE	SIMPLE PAST	PAST PARTICIPLE
to rain	rained	rained
to smoke	smoked	smoked
to talk	talked	talked
to start	started	started
to clean	cleaned	cleaned
to borrow	borrowed	borrowed
to wait	waited	waited

Irregular

INFINITIVE	SIMPLE PAST	PAST PARTICIPLE
to have	had	had
to drive	drove	driven
to drink	drank	drunk
to hang	hung	hung
to make	made	made
to send	sent	sent
to eat	ate	eaten
to buy	bought	bought
to give	gave	given

1. We _____ (to eat) our breakfast, so we were hungry.

2. She _____ (to clean) the fridge, so I cleaned it for her.

3. It _____ (to rain), so the streets were dry.

4. She _____ (to drive) on icy roads before, so she had a bad accident.

5. My husband _____ (to hang) the clothes on the clothesline, so I did it when I got home.

6. You _____ (to talk) about that before today.

7. I _____ (to buy) butter, so I went to the store again.

8. We _____ (to send) the check, so we sent it this morning.

9. She _____ (to have) her shower, so I left without her.

10. They _____ (to borrow) enough money, so we lent them $1,000.

11. He _____ (to give) me his address.

12. I _____ (to wait) a long time before it arrived in the mail.

13. My uncle _____ (to smoke) in three years, and he started again.

14. He _____ (to drink) his juice, so I drank it.

15. The movie _____ (to start), so we went to buy some chocolates and candies.

16. My wife _____ (to make) supper, so we went to a restaurant.

The Past Perfect Tense: Question Form

Place **had** before the subject to create the question form of the past perfect tense. The past participle of the verb is used when forming questions in the past perfect tense.

I had worked →	had I worked →	Had I worked with you?
you had worked →	had you worked →	Had you worked in Mexico?
he had worked →	had he worked →	Had he worked for his father?
she had worked →	had she worked →	Had she worked in the city?
it had worked →	had it worked →	Had it worked well?
we had worked →	had we worked →	Had we worked together?
they had worked →	had they worked →	Had they worked late?

The past participle of all regular verbs is the same as the simple past tense form (add -**ed**).

INFINITIVE	SIMPLE PAST	PAST PARTICIPLE
to plan	planned	planned
to live	lived	lived
to end	ended	ended
to happen	happened	happened
to taste	tasted	tasted
to try	tried	tried

The past participle of all irregular verbs has a different form and must be studied and learned. Refer to Lesson 44.

INFINITIVE	SIMPLE PAST	PAST PARTICIPLE
to withdraw	withdrew	withdrawn
to know	knew	known
to speak	spoke	spoken
to see	saw	seen
to make	made	made
to have	had	had
to wear	wore	worn
to give	gave	given

*Rewrite the following sentences to create the question form of the past perfect tense by placing **had** before the subject. Use the past participle of the verb in parentheses. You have already learned these verbs in previous exercises. Don't forget to include a question mark (?) in your answer.*

1. He (to know) that you were my brother.

   _____

2. They (to withdraw) all the money from their savings account.

   _____

3. You (to try) to ski before you bought the skis.

   _____

4. The play (to end) when she arrived.

   _____

5. You (to give) him your phone number.

   _____

6. Your aunt (to wear) this dress before.

   _____

7. They (to taste) seafood before today.

   _____

8. Richard and Jennifer (to plan) their vacation together.

   _____

9. Wade (to make) coffee for everybody.

   _____

10. You (to have) your breakfast before you went to school.

    _____

11. The teacher (to speak) to you before she called your parents.

    _____

12. It (to happen) before.

    _____

13. You (to see) that woman before she came to your house.

    _____

14. They (to live) in Ontario before they moved to British Columbia.

    _____

Rewrite the sentences that follow to create the question form of the past perfect tense. Place **had** *before the subject, and use the past participle of the verb in parentheses. You have already learned these verbs in previous exercises. Don't forget to include a question mark (?) in your answer.*

Regular

INFINITIVE	SIMPLE PAST	PAST PARTICIPLE
to realize	realized	realized
to play	played	played
to work	worked	worked
to notice	noticed	noticed
to belong	belonged	belonged
to seem	seemed	seemed

Irregular

INFINITIVE	SIMPLE PAST	PAST PARTICIPLE
to take	took	taken
to find	found	found
to leave	left	left
to take	took	taken
to read	read	read
to pay	paid	paid
to be	was/were	been
to bring	brought	brought

1. She (to realize) what she did.

   _____

2. You (to take) the wrong bus.

   _____

3. It (to seem) fair to everyone.

   _____

4. Your boss (to bring) his dog to work before today.

   _____

5. Tony (to be) in the hospital before he had his operation.

   _____

6. They (to leave) the building before the fire started.

   _____

7. Jessica (to work) as a flight attendant before she became a nurse.

   _____

8. He (to take) the time to do it right.

   _____

9. They (to notice) where you put it.

_____

10. You (to pay) cash for it.

_____

11. Maria (to find) a new job before she quit her old job.

_____

12. He (to play) hockey before he joined our team.

_____

13. You (to read) the contract before you signed it.

_____

14. It (to belong) to your grandmother before your mother gave it to you.

_____

Answer Key

1 To Be: Present Tense

1-1 1. The girl is pretty. 2. I am ready. 3. She is my friend. 4. They are twins. 5. The flowers are yellow. 6. The flashlight is in the tent. 7. The fridge and counter in the kitchen are dirty. 8. I am tired today. 9. We are busy. 10. The toys are in the basement. 11. The ribbons in my hair are pink. 12. The kitchen is very small. 13. The vacuum is in the closet. 14. He is nice. 15. The microwave oven is in the kitchen. 16. The toy is on the floor. 17. I am sick today.

1-2 1. is 2. are 3. is 4. are 5. are 6. are 7. are 8. are 9. is 10. are 11. is 12. is 13. are 14. is 15. is 16. are 17. is 18. is 19. am 20. is 21. is 22. is 23. is 24. is 25. are 26. is 27. is 28. is 29. is 30. is 31. is 32. is 33. is 34. is

2 To Be: Present Tense: Negative Form

2-1 1. The cheese is not on the table. The cheese isn't on the table. 2. She is not my sister. She isn't my sister. 3. My neighbors are not Spanish. My neighbors aren't Spanish. 4. My sister-in-law is not Italian. My sister-in-law isn't Italian. 5. Diane is not pregnant. Diane isn't pregnant. 6. The limes are not sour. The limes aren't sour. 7. The bus is not empty. The bus isn't empty. 8. The kids are not early for class today. The kids aren't early for class today. 9. The drawers are not empty. The drawers aren't empty. 10. It is not a nice city. It isn't a nice city.

2-2 1. isn't 2. aren't 3. isn't 4. aren't 5. isn't 6. isn't 7. aren't 8. aren't 9. aren't 10. isn't 11. isn't 12. isn't 13. aren't 14. aren't 15. isn't 16. isn't 17. isn't 18. aren't 19. isn't 20. aren't 21. aren't 22. isn't 23. aren't 24. isn't 25. isn't 26. isn't 27. am not 28. isn't 29. isn't 30. isn't 31. aren't 32. aren't 33. isn't 34. isn't

3 To Be: Present Tense: Question Form

3-1 1. Are the wheels in the garage? 2. Is the sharpener on my desk? 3. Is the woman very poor? 4. Are the toothbrush and toothpaste in the bathroom? 5. Is my bathing suit on the clothesline? 6. Am I in your English class? 7. Is it cold outside? 8. Is he a policeman in the city? 9. Are the coats on the floor? 10. Are Johanne and Véronique in a meeting? 11. Are the toys in the box downstairs? 12. Are the cow and calf brown? 13. Is the orange juice sweet? 14. Are the frogs in the pond? 15. Is the goldfish in the bowl? 16. Are you serious? 17. Is Marie French?

3-2 1. Is 2. Are 3. Are 4. Is 5. Are 6. Is 7. Are 8. Is 9. Are 10. Are 11. Is 12. Am 13. Are 14. Is 15. Is 16. Are 17. Are 18. Is 19. Are 20. Are 21. Are 22. Is 23. Are 24. Is 25. Is 26. Are 27. Are 28. Is 29. Is 30. Is 31. Are 32. Am

4 To Be: Past Tense

4-1 1. Joanie and Isabelle were at the beach. 2. He was my roommate. 3. It was in my pocket. 4. The snake was in the garden. 5. The diapers were in the bag. 6. She was a hairdresser. 7. Lisa was sick. 8. The kids were in the pool. 9. The bucket was full of minnows. 10. The washer and dryer were in the laundry room. 11. I was in my office. 12. The pencil was on the floor. 13. Sorry that I was late. 14. The flowers were for Jennifer. 15. My grandmother was in the hospital. 16. The exam was easy. 17. The crust was very thick. 18. The farm was very far.

4-2 1. was 2. were 3. was 4. were 5. was 6. was 7. was 8. was 9. were 10. were 11. was 12. was 13. were 14. was 15. were 16. was 17. were 18. was 19. were 20. was 21. were 22. was 23. were 24. was 25. were 26. was 27. was 28. were 29. was 30. was 31. were 32. were

5 To Be: Past Tense: Negative Form

5-1 1. The dress was not blue. The dress wasn't blue. 2. The couch in the living room was not dirty. The couch in the living room wasn't dirty. 3. They were not very fast. They weren't very fast. 4. It was not a good joke. It wasn't a good joke. 5. The raccoons were not in the tree. The raccoons weren't in the tree. 6. The slippers were not purple. The slippers weren't purple. 7. We were not at the play last night. We weren't at the play last night. 8. The plates were not in the dishwasher. The plates weren't in the dishwasher. 9. Karen was not a waitress for three years. Karen wasn't a waitress for three years. 10. My name was not on the list. My name wasn't on the list.

5-2 1. weren't 2. wasn't 3. wasn't 4. weren't 5. weren't 6. wasn't 7. wasn't 8. weren't 9. weren't 10. wasn't 11. wasn't 12. wasn't 13. wasn't 14. wasn't 15. weren't 16. wasn't 17. weren't 18. wasn't 19. weren't 20. wasn't 21. wasn't 22. wasn't 23. weren't 24. wasn't 25. wasn't 26. wasn't 27. weren't 28. wasn't 29. wasn't 30. wasn't 31. wasn't 32. wasn't

6 To Be: Past Tense: Question Form

6-1 1. Was it free? 2. Was the airplane very low in the sky? 3. Was the mall empty? 4. Were they in kindergarten together? 5. Was it bitter? 6. Were you angry at Susan? 7. Was the recipe easy? 8. Were the nail clippers in the drawer? 9. Were the curtains velvet? 10. Was the tablecloth dirty? 11. Was it enough? 12. Was she a flight attendant when she was young? 13. Were the ashtrays full? 14. Was the lady thin? 15. Was Claude seasick on the ship? 16. Were the crutches behind the door?

6-2 1. Was 2. Were 3. Was 4. Were 5. Was 6. Were 7. Was 8. Were 9. Was 10. Was 11. Was 12. Was 13. Were 14. Was 15. Were 16. Was 17. Were 18. Was 19. Were 20. Were 21. Was 22. Was 23. Were 24. Was 25. Was 26. Was 27. Was 28. Was 29. Was 30. Was 31. Were 32. Was

7 Exceptional Uses with the Verb To Be

7-1 1. My daughter is afraid of the dark. 2. Is Jason right? 3. She wasn't hungry for breakfast this morning. 4. Please open the windows. I am very hot. 5. I am not ashamed of the size of my shoes. 6. Cathy was thirty-three years old on her last birthday. 7. We were very thirsty after the race. 8. You are wrong again. 9. I am not right all the time. 10. Are you scared of thunder? 11. He wasn't afraid of the lightning. 12. I was cold this morning. 13. Are the guests hungry? 14. My mother and father were ashamed of my behavior. 15. Is your son scared of spiders? 16. I am not eighteen years old. 17. Bill is happy because he is right. 18. I am cold because of the snowballs in my pocket.

7-2 1. wasn't 2. Were 3. isn't 4. were 5. is 6. was 7. isn't 8. am 9. isn't 10. is 11. Was 12. is 13. Are 14. Was 15. Was 16. weren't 17. isn't 18. Were 19. wasn't 20. aren't 21. is 22. Was 23. aren't 24. am 25. are 26. Were 27. wasn't 28. is 29. isn't 30. was 31. is 32. Is 33. wasn't 34. are

8 Adjectives

8-1 1. The cute little house is for sale.   2. It is a very sharp knife.   3. He is a tall, handsome man.   4. It was a cold, windy day yesterday.   5. I want a black leather jacket.   6. They drink prune juice every morning.   7. The big, green bug is in my shoe.   8. Elizabeth is a French teacher.   9. The ugly, hairy spider is in the kitchen.   10. Canada is a big, beautiful country.   11. The English test was hard.   12. He was a nice policeman.   13. Look at the beautiful white snow.   14. The little green frog is in the pond.   15. It was a huge whale.

8-2 1. It was a long, hard winter.   2. I need a new silver watch.   3. My right hand is sore.   4. I want the round balloons.   5. We like to watch old movies.   6. Look at the bright stars in the sky.   7. I like BBQ chips.   8. They want chocolate cake for dessert.   9. I love Mexican food.   10. He is a wealthy lawyer.   11. You draw funny pictures.   12. It was a long, boring meeting.   13. My left knee is swollen.   14. The kids like junk food.   15. We like to make rhubarb pies.   16. I hate strawberry yogurt.   17. We wear white shoes to school.   18. They are identical twins.

9 To *Have*: Present Tense

9-1 1. He has a bad attitude.   2. The cat has white paws.   3. I have a peanut butter sandwich for lunch today.   4. Maria has a red velvet skirt.   5. We have a nice landlord.   6. Jessica has a terrible headache.   7. We have a good housekeeper.   8. She has a lot of dandruff.   9. Tony has very good skills.   10. The milk has a weird taste.   11. The house has a green roof.   12. It has a short tail.   13. We have a day off next week.   14. I have a warm sleeping bag.   15. My sister has purple eye shadow.   16. You have a nice smile.

9-2 1. have   2. has   3. has   4. have   5. has   6. have   7. has   8. has   9. has   10. have   11. has   12. has   13. has   14. have   15. have   16. has   17. has   18. has   19. have   20. have   21. has   22. have   23. has   24. have   25. has   26. have   27. has   28. has   29. has   30. have   31. has   32. has

10 To *Have*: Present Tense: Negative Form

10-1 1. My cat does not have fleas. My cat doesn't have fleas.   2. We do not have a satellite dish on the roof. We don't have a satellite dish on the roof.   3. I do not have a surprise for you. I don't have a surprise for you.   4. Jimmy does not have a fast snowmobile. Jimmy doesn't have a fast snowmobile.   5. We do not have many good books about antique jewelry. We don't have many good books about antique jewelry.   6. She does not have a lot of customers. She doesn't have a lot of customers.   7. My brother-in-law does not have a screwdriver. My brother-in-law doesn't have a screwdriver.   8. The clown does not have a big red nose. The clown doesn't have a big red nose.   9. I do not have long straight hair and bangs. I don't have long straight hair and bangs.   10. She does not have fantastic news. She doesn't have fantastic news.

10-2 1. don't   2. doesn't   3. doesn't   4. doesn't   5. don't   6. doesn't   7. don't   8. don't   9. don't   10. doesn't   11. don't   12. doesn't   13. doesn't   14. don't   15. doesn't   16. doesn't   17. don't   18. doesn't   19. don't   20. doesn't   21. don't   22. doesn't   23. doesn't   24. don't   25. doesn't   26. don't   27. don't   28. don't   29. don't   30. don't   31. don't   32. don't   33. doesn't   34. doesn't

11 To *Have*: Present Tense: Question Form

11-1 1. Do you have a pink eraser?   2. Does he have my phone number?   3. Do they have everything they need?   4. Do we have the same scarf?   5. Do I have rights?   6. Does Marissa have green flip-flops?   7. Do you have a huge turkey for Thanksgiving?   8. Do they have a lease until next year?   9. Does it have a funny taste?   10. Do you have two important appointments today?   11. Does the dove have white wings?   12. Do we have a day off next week?   13. Does David have a pager?   14. Does Juanita have a good recipe for meat loaf?   15. Do we have a tight deadline for the project?   16. Do they have a big celebration on Christmas Eve?

11-2 1. Do   2. Do   3. Does   4. Do   5. Does   6. Do   7. Does   8. Do   9. Does   10. Does   11. Do   12. Do   13. Does   14. Do   15. Does   16. Does   17. Does   18. Does   19. Do   20. Do   21. Does   22. Do   23. Does   24. Do   25. Does   26. Do   27. Do   28. Do   29. Do   30. Do   31. Do   32. Does

12 The Simple Present Tense

12-1   1. He smokes American cigarettes.   2. Karen blushes when she sees that boy.   3. I love caramel apple cake.   4. He cries like a baby.   5. It amazes me.   6. It jumps very high.   7. He kisses all the girls in school.   8. My cats scratch the furniture.   9. They help many people in the village.   10. The knights guard the king and castle in the kingdom.   11. He never flushes the toilet.

12-2   1. explains   2. whisper   3. crushes   4. buys   5. do   6. earn   7. works   8. manages   9. carry   10. owe   11. eats   12. fears   13. follow   14. work   15. drinks   16. pushes   17. spoils   18. dreams   19. drives   20. does   21. goes   22. own   23. obey   24. melts

13 The Simple Present Tense: Negative Form

13-1   1. My husband does not snore every night. My husband doesn't snore every night.   2. I do not believe your story about the giant monkeys. I don't believe your story about the giant monkeys.   3. Nancy and Yvan do not collect coins. Nancy and Yvan don't collect coins.   4. She does not speak several foreign languages. She doesn't speak several foreign languages.   5. It does not dislike fish. It doesn't dislike fish.   6. Ron does not swear and yell in class. Ron doesn't swear and yell in class.   7. Sara does not sell sewing machines. Sara doesn't sell sewing machines.   8. I do not trust you. I don't trust you.   9. We do not eat meat. We don't eat meat.

13-2   1. doesn't   2. don't   3. don't   4. doesn't   5. don't   6. doesn't   7. doesn't   8. don't   9. doesn't   10. don't   11. doesn't   12. doesn't   13. don't   14. don't   15. doesn't   16. don't   17. doesn't   18. don't   19. doesn't   20. doesn't   21. doesn't   22. don't   23. doesn't   24. doesn't   25. don't   26. don't   27. doesn't   28. doesn't   29. don't   30. doesn't

14 The Simple Present Tense: Question Form

14-1   1. Does she skate in the morning?   2. Do they boil the vegetables?   3. Does he sleep in the afternoon?   4. Do the boys play chess at night?   5. Do you pay the mortgage on time?   6. Does she read the English newspaper?   7. Do they drive to work together?   8. Does it cost $20 to travel by train to the city?   9. Does she scream when she watches horror movies?   10. Does she want a new hobby?   11. Does the king wear a red velvet crown?   12. Does Bobby play with toy soldiers?   13. Do you put salt and pepper in the dough?   14. Does Jackie touch everything in my office?   15. Do you see the fox in the woods?

14-2   1. Does   2. Do   3. Does   4. Do   5. Do   6. Does   7. Do   8. Does   9. Do   10. Do   11. Does   12. Do   13. Does   14. Does   15. Do   16. Does   17. Does   18. Do   19. Do   20. Does   21. Does   22. Do   23. Does   24. Do   25. Does   26. Do   27. Do   28. Does

15 Possessive Pronouns

15-1   1. She visits her relatives every summer.   2. We hide our money under the carpet in the master bedroom.   3. They keep their jewels in a jewelry box.   4. I wash my stairs with a sponge.   5. He passes all his exams.   6. She dresses her dolls in pink.   7. I open my mail after breakfast.   8. He bites his nails.   9. We rent our apartment.   10. It licks its paws.   11. I burn my marshmallows.   12. Jeff takes his pills in the morning.   13. The boys forget their homework every day.   14. He wipes his nose on his sleeve.   15. She dyes her hair.   16. The sailors believe their new submarine is better.

15-2   1. their   2. her   3. our   4. my   5. her   6. your   7. my   8. its   9. our   10. his   11. their   12. my   13. their   14. his   15. our   16. his   17. my   18. her   19. their   20. my   21. her   22. your   23. our   24. her   25. his   26. my

16 The Simple Past Tense

16-1   1. I used my hair dryer to dry my hair.   2. We tried a new recipe last night.   3. Thomas answered the phone.   4. I noticed that your sweater was inside out.   5. The car landed upside down in the ditch. 6. She shared her snack with her friends at school yesterday.   7. The minimum wage increased last year. 8. Suzanne lied about her age.   9. My company signed the lease for our building for another three years. 10. The teacher challenged her students and rewarded them for their hard work.   11. The eel killed the toad.

16-2   1. accepted   2. joined   3. moved   4. knocked   5. described   6. proved   7. denied   8. borrowed 9. watched   10. used   11. tidied   12. rained   13. painted   14. avoided   15. pushed   16. married 17. pleased   18. destroyed   19. served   20. obtained   21. arrested   22. ordered   23. decided 24. expected

17   The Simple Past Tense with Irregular Verbs: 1

17-1   1. She blew on her soup because it was hot.   2. The house shook a lot during the earthquake.   3. They took the plane and spent their honeymoon overseas.   4. I always felt sick when I was pregnant.   5. He tore his pants when he fell.   6. We bought a nice gift for our grandparents in Ireland.   7. The kids slid down the mountain on their new toboggan.   8. I did the dishes after supper.   9. I cut my finger on the sharp saw.   10. You broke my favorite cup.   11. Your dog bit my ankle.   12. Karen found a purse at the beach. 13. I taught math at the high school last year.

17-2   1. spoke   2. began   3. gave   4. hung   5. saw   6. sat   7. stole   8. paid   9. drew   10. swore 11. dug   12. held   13. shot   14. heard   15. left   16. saw

18   The Simple Past Tense with Irregular Verbs: 2

18-1   1. We withdrew enough money for the whole month.   2. I caught a bullfrog and four tadpoles in the pond.   3. Salina rode a horse for the first time yesterday.   4. Robert, Claire, and Daniel built a huge sand castle on the beach.   5. Brandon bent the hanger to open the car door.   6. I drove to the post office to buy some stamps and envelopes.   7. The hunter forgot his rifle in the woods.   8. You woke your grandmother when you knocked on the window.   9. The sheep and lamb slept on the hay in the barn.   10. I had a bagel with bacon, tomato, cheese, and lettuce for lunch.   11. Camilie understood what the teacher taught in class today.   12. My mother froze the vegetables for the winter.   13. Dimitri lent the shovel to his neighbor. 14. The red team beat the blue team.   15. Laurent came to help us with the inventory in the warehouse.

18-2   1. brought   2. cost   3. rose   4. won   5. grew   6. put   7. meant   8. shut   9. chose   10. forgave 11. thought   12. lost   13. hurt   14. kept   15. sent   16. drank

19   The Simple Past Tense with Irregular Verbs: 3

19-1   1. She sang on Monday, Wednesday, and Friday at the concert in Montreal.   2. The house was dark because of the power failure, so we lit the candles.   3. The car spun out of control on the ice.   4. I read the newspaper in the evening on Saturday and Sunday.   5. My son fought at school on Tuesday and Thursday last week.   6. The phone rang in the middle of the night.   7. I knew that he was guilty of the crime. 8. She met Sara at the liquor store.   9. Sorry, but I ate all the icing on your cake when you went to the bathroom.   10. I got a big raise at work last month.   11. We sold our parrot because he was too noisy. 12. Alexandre threw the papers in the fire.   13. My pants fit me last year.   14. Carmen ran and hid under the bed.   15. We fed meat to the fox.

19-2   1. dealt   2. said   3. swept   4. made   5. stuck   6. hit   7. became, quit   8. wore   9. led   10. flew 11. wrote   12. swam   13. wept   14. told   15. stood   16. gave

20   The Simple Past Tense: Negative Form

20-1   1. They did not watch the hockey game on their new big-screen TV. They didn't watch the hockey game on their new big-screen TV.   2. I did not forget to tell him. I didn't forget to tell him.   3. She did not waste my valuable time. She didn't waste my valuable time.   4. Marcia did not report her income. Marcia didn't report her income.   5. I did not shake the bottle of medicine. I didn't shake the bottle of medicine.   6. My uncle did not shave his head. My uncle didn't shave his head.   7. He did not apologize to his friend. He didn't apologize to his friend.   8. We did not find clams and mussels in the sand on the beach. We didn't find clams and mussels in the sand on the beach.   9. The police did not read the man his rights. The police didn't read the man his rights.   10. It did not scratch my skin. It didn't scratch my skin.

20-2   1. He didn't prevent the accident.   2. She didn't express her opinion.   3. The movie didn't last three hours.   4. They didn't go to see their granddaughter and grandson.   5. They didn't save a lot of money for their trip to Greece.   6. Patricia didn't lose her mittens, scarf, and hat at school.   7. Sonia didn't translate the letter.   8. I didn't buy a gift for her.   9. Mario didn't find a black leather wallet in the snow.   10. We didn't put the leftovers in plastic bags. 11. I didn't tear my pantyhose. 12. I didn't know you were there. 13. He didn't deposit his pay in his savings account. 14. The plumber didn't fix the pipes, shower, and toilet in the bathroom upstairs. 15. I didn't clean the litter box and brush the cat this morning. 16. I didn't read my horoscope today. 17. The wind didn't bend the antenna. 18. Laura didn't grow two inches and gain ten pounds last year.

21 The Simple Past Tense: Question Form

21-1 1. Did you see the beautiful rainbow? 2. Did he offend you when he said that? 3. Did Jessica find a starfish on the beach? 4. Did the squirrel eat the peanuts? 5. Did he shoot a deer last weekend? 6. Did I indicate my overtime hours on my timesheet? 7. Did they remain friends after the argument? 8. Did Luke break the remote control for the TV? 9. Did she change her mind? 10. Did Brandon cheat when we played cards? 11. Did they weigh the fish on the scale? 12. Did you put garlic in the salad? 13. Did the people elect a new president? 14. Did he escape from prison? 15. Did it sleep under your bed?

21-2 1. Did you take a picture of the sunset? 2. Did she lock the safe? 3. Did they attend the funeral? 4. Did Barry order seafood? 5. Did the chipmunk climb the tree? 6. Did they ride the roller-coaster? 7. Did she make the earrings? 8. Did the divers find a treasure chest? 9. Did the baby blow bubbles in the bath? 10. Did they load the wagon? 11. Did the rattlesnake bite his arm? 12. Did the policeman put handcuffs on the thief? 13. Did she convince you? 14. Did you pick a flower for me? 15. Did it appear to be true? 16. Did you ask a question? 17. Did the maid iron my apron? 18. Did the dog lick my ice-cream cone? 19. Did she draw a picture of a mermaid? 20. Did Ravi lose his comb?

22 Prepositions: *In* and *On*

22-1 1. The garbage can is in the garage. 2. Do you see signs of life on the moon? 3. We will talk about it in the morning. 4. Mark moved here in 1997. 5. Don't throw your empty bottle on the ground. 6. We spent five days in Paris. 7. All the kids start school in September. 8. I will see you on Saturday. 9. They advertised it on the radio in California. 10. What do you have in your mouth? 11. I saw your picture in the newspaper in Ontario. 12. It's my birthday on Tuesday. 13. The bathroom is on the left. 14. We went for a ride on his motorcycle in the country. 15. She presented her project on trees.

22-2 1. on 2. in 3. in 4. on 5. on 6. in 7. on 8. on 9. in 10. on 11. on 12. on 13. in 14. in 15. on 16. in 17. in 18. in 19. in 20. in 21. on 22. in 23. on 24. in 25. on 26. in 27. on 28. in 29. on 30. in 31. on 32. on 33. on 34. in 35. on 36. in 37. on 38. on 39. in 40. in

23 *There Is* and *There Are*: Present Tense

23-1 1. There are many meatballs and red peppers in the sauce. 2. There is a whiteboard in my classroom. 3. There are rocks in my boot. 4. There is a phone book on her desk. 5. There are gigantic footprints in the snow. 6. There is a fire hydrant at the corner of my street. 7. There are many caterpillars on the tree. 8. There is a black stallion in the field. 9. There are four piglets and three colts in the barn. 10. There is a quilt on my bed. 11. There are many seagulls on the beach. 12. There is a new keyboard in the box. 13. There are two sponges in the bucket. 14. There are many dirty plates in the sink. 15. There are six diamonds on my ring. 16. There are a few gray squirrels in the tree.

23-2 1. are 2. is 3. is 4. is 5. are 6. is 7. is 8. is 9. are 10. is 11. are 12. is 13. is 14. are 15. is 16. is 17. are 18. is 19. are 20. is 21. are 22. is 23. are 24. is 25. are 26. is 27. is 28. are 29. is 30. are

24 *There Is* and *There Are*: Present Tense: Negative Form

24-1 1. There is not a lot of shade in the backyard. There isn't a lot of shade in the backyard. 2. There are not three gold buttons on my coat. There aren't three gold buttons on my coat. 3. There are not two yellow folders on my desk. There aren't two yellow folders on my desk. 4. There is not a tricycle on the sidewalk. There isn't a tricycle on the sidewalk. 5. There is not a thermometer in the bathroom. There isn't a thermometer in the bathroom. 6. There are not three white rabbits in the cage. There aren't three white rabbits in the cage. 7. There is not a turtle on the log. There isn't a turtle on the log. 8. There are not many angels in the picture. There aren't many angels in the picture.   9. There is not a scarecrow in the field. There isn't a scarecrow in the field.   10. There are not many dimes and nickels in the wishing well. There aren't many dimes and nickels in the wishing well.   11. There are not five quarters and a penny in my back pocket. There aren't five quarters and a penny in my back pocket.

24-2   1. isn't   2. isn't   3. aren't   4. isn't   5. aren't   6. isn't   7. isn't   8. isn't   9. aren't   10. isn't   11. isn't   12. aren't   13. isn't   14. aren't   15. isn't   16. aren't   17. isn't   18. aren't   19. isn't   20. isn't   21. isn't   22. aren't   23. isn't   24. aren't   25. isn't   26. aren't   27. isn't   28. isn't   29. aren't   30. isn't   31. aren't

25   *There Is* and *There Are*: Present Tense: Question Form

25-1   1. Is there a vending machine in the cafeteria?   2. Are there enough life jackets in the boat?   3. Are there many skyscrapers in the city?   4. Is there a lifeguard at the pool?   5. Are there two owls in the tree?   6. Is there a diving board at the public pool?   7. Are there germs on my hands?   8. Is there a handle on my suitcase?   9. Is there a UFO in the sky?   10. Are there aliens in the UFO?   11. Are there candy canes on the Christmas tree?   12. Is there a ruler on my desk?   13. Are there enough place mats on the table?   14. Is there a measuring cup in the cupboard?   15. Is there a catfish in the pail?   16. Are there many hangers in the closet?   17. Is there a mirror in your purse?

25-2   1. Are   2. Is   3. Is   4. Are   5. Is   6. Is   7. Are   8. Is   9. Is   10. Are   11. Are   12. Are   13. Is   14. Is   15. Are   16. Are   17. Is   18. Is   19. Are   20. Is   21. Are   22. Are   23. Is   24. Are   25. Is   26. Are   27. Is   28. Is   29. Is   30. Are   31. Are   32. Is   33. Is   34. Are

26   *There Is* and *There Are*: Past Tense

26-1   1. There was rust on the knife.   2. There were rules to follow.   3. There was a big sale at the mall, so I bought a scarf and shoes.   4. There was a CD player in my car, but someone stole it.   5. There were wet towels on the floor after he took his shower.   6. There was a hurricane in the southeast last week.   7. There were many stray cats in the alley.   8. There were beautiful fireworks in the sky last night.   9. There was a magnifying glass on the table.   10. There were two circles, three squares, and four triangles in the picture.   11. There was a diamond in her belly button.   12. There was a cork in the bottle of wine.   13. There were many straws in the cup on the counter in the kitchen.   14. There was a good story about you in the newspaper this morning.   15. There were a lot of dirty pots and pans in the sink.   16. There were many dimes, nickels, and quarters in my piggy bank.   17. There was gravy on my mashed potatoes but not on my meat.   18. There was a snowstorm in the northwest last night.

26-2   1. was   2. were   3. were   4. was   5. were   6. was   7. were   8. was   9. were   10. was   11. was   12. was   13. were   14. were   15. was   16. were   17. was   18. were   19. was   20. were   21. were   22. was   23. was   24. was   25. was   26. were   27. was   28. were   29. was   30. were   31. wcrc   32. were   33. was   34. was

27   *There Is* and *There Are*: Past Tense: Negative Form

27-1   1. There was not a crack in my windshield. There wasn't a crack in my windshield.   2. There were not many shells and stones in the sand on the beach. There weren't many shells and stones in the sand on the beach.   3. There were not a lot of big heavy trucks on the bridge this morning. There weren't a lot of big heavy trucks on the bridge this morning.   4. There was not a peach in my lunch box. There wasn't a peach in my lunch box.   5. There were not two staplers on my desk in my office. There weren't two staplers on my desk in my office.   6. There was not a big brown beaver near the dam. There wasn't a big brown beaver near the dam.   7. There were not many wheelchairs in the hall in the hospital. There weren't many wheelchairs in the hall in the hospital.   8. There was not a wreath on the door. There wasn't a wreath on the door.   9. There were not many camels in the desert. There weren't many camels in the desert.   10. There was not a huge octopus in the boat. There wasn't a huge octopus in the boat.   11. There were not many fun games to play. There weren't many fun games to play.

27-2   1. wasn't   2. weren't   3. wasn't   4. weren't   5. wasn't   6. wasn't   7. weren't   8. wasn't   9. weren't   10. wasn't   11. wasn't   12. weren't   13. weren't   14. wasn't   15. weren't   16. wasn't   17. wasn't   18. wasn't   19. weren't   20. wasn't   21. weren't   22. weren't   23. weren't   24. weren't   25. wasn't   26. wasn't   27. weren't   28. wasn't   29. wasn't   30. wasn't   31. wasn't   32. weren't

28 *There Is* and *There Are*: Past Tense: Question Form

28-1 1. Were there many knights to guard the castle in the kingdom?   2. Was there a wooden outhouse behind our cottage in the country?   3. Was there a picture of a skull and bones on the bottle?   4. Were there many cigarette butts in the ashtray?   5. Was there a car in my blind spot?   6. Were there pink fuzzy dice on his rearview mirror?   7. Was there a splinter in his thumb?   8. Was there enough room on the bus for everybody?   9. Was there a rude boy in your class last year?   10. Were there two pretty blue bows in her hair?   11. Was there a Canada goose near the lake?   12. Was there a green carpet on the floor in the entrance?   13. Was there a lot of garlic in the butter?   14. Were there many people without a passport at the airport?   15. Were there many thorns on the rose?   16. Was there a garage sale last weekend?   17. Were there many people on the roller-coaster?   18. Was there a locksmith in the mall?

28-2 1. Were   2. Was   3. Was   4. Was   5. Was   6. Was   7. Was   8. Were   9. Were   10. Was   11. Was   12. Was   13. Were   14. Was   15. Was   16. Were   17. Were   18. Was   19. Were   20. Was   21. Were   22. Was   23. Was   24. Was   25. Was   26. Were   27. Was   28. Was   29. Were   30. Was   31. Was   32. Was   33. Were   34. Was

29 Prepositions: *To* and *At*

29-1 1. Please explain this to me.   2. The girls ate cake at the birthday party.   3. We saw Tony and his brother at the restaurant.   4. I sold my car to Mike.   5. I bought a muzzle for my dog at the pet store.   6. The funeral was at four o'clock.   7. We fed the apple cores to the raccoons.   8. I go to the gym daily.   9. We made a bonfire at the beach.   10. They drive to the city.   11. The elevator went to the basement.   12. We noticed that there was a policeman at the door.   13. He talked to the press after the meeting.   14. They gave the prize to my opponent.   15. Call me at 6:30 P.M.   16. We went to England and Spain last year.

29-2 1. at   2. at   3. to   4. at   5. at   6. to   7. to   8. at   9. at, at   10. to   11. to   12. to   13. at   14. to   15. to   16. at   17. to   18. at   19. to   20. at   21. to   22. at   23. to   24. to   25. at   26. to   27. at   28. at   29. to   30. at   31. to   32. at   33. at   34. to

30 The Present Progressive (Continuous) Tense

30-1 1. The wolf is howling at the moon.   2. Sheila is worrying now because her daughter is late.   3. It is cold. We are shivering and we have goose bumps.   4. They are crossing the lake in a canoe.   5. The mayor is discussing the enormous potholes on the roads.   6. She is pouring a soft drink for you.   7. The nuns are sewing clothes and knitting slippers for the children.   8. The policeman is wearing his bulletproof vest.   9. My great-grandfather is living in a retirement home.   10. They are suing the city.   11. We are looking at the Big Dipper and the Little Dipper with our binoculars.   12. Rollande is drinking water because she has the hiccups.   13. My stepfather is repairing the bleachers in the stadium.   14. It is snowing again.   15. The dog is barking and growling at the groundhog outside.

30-2 1. is dressing   2. are coughing   3. is tickling   4. am rewinding   5. is waving   6. is rubbing   7. is drooling   8. are sitting   9. are living   10. is delivering   11. are writing   12. is whispering   13. are breaking   14. is ringing   15. is winning   16. are rattling   17. is teasing   18. are annoying   19. is curling   20. are wasting   21. is juggling   22. is overflowing   23. is chewing   24. is putting   25. am sending   26. are surrounding   27. am leaving   28. is drawing   29. are melting   30. am giving

31 The Present Progressive (Continuous) Tense: Negative Form

31-1 1. He is not shouting at you. He isn't shouting at you.   2. They are not waiting downstairs for us. They aren't waiting downstairs for us.   3. The ship is not sinking. The ship isn't sinking.   4. The dog is not burying the bone in the sand. The dog isn't burying the bone in the sand.   5. We are not planting the seeds in the garden. We aren't planting the seeds in the garden.   6. I am not teaching in the elementary school this year. No contraction.   7. Mike is not stirring the paint with the paintbrush. Mike isn't stirring the paint with the paintbrush.   8. You are not wearing your seat belt. You aren't wearing your seat belt.   9. The crowd is not clapping and cheering. The crowd isn't clapping and cheering.

31-2 1. isn't joking   2. aren't praying   3. aren't dancing   4. am not making   5. isn't putting   6. aren't dripping   7. isn't wiggling   8. aren't walking   9. isn't squeezing   10. am not separating   11. aren't ending   12. isn't correcting   13. aren't complaining   14. isn't boring   15. isn't aiming   16. aren't solving   17. isn't working   18. am not starring   19. isn't winking   20. aren't freeing   21. isn't surrendering   22. aren't wrapping   23. isn't swallowing   24. isn't sharpening   25. isn't typing   26. aren't inviting

32 The Present Progressive (Continuous) Tense: Question Form

32-1   1. Are they talking about the newborn baby?   2. Is he hunting with a bow and arrow?   3. Is the saleslady offering you a good deal?   4. Is it walking backward or forward?   5. Are the employees adding their expenses for the business trip?   6. Is Mrs. Smith living in the suburbs?   7. Is Mr. Jones working in a gas station?   8. Is he slicing the pineapple?   9. Am I rocking the boat?   10. Is she sweating a lot?   11. Is my lip bleeding?   12. Are you bringing your compass when we go in the woods?   13. Are Bob and Tina on the beach enjoying the sunrise?   14. Am I eating your muffin?   15. Is Rosa making a cake for the surprise birthday party?

32-2   1. Is Tom spying on us?   2. Is he pushing the kids in the wheelbarrow?   3. Is the patient suffering a lot?   4. Is she cutting the crusty bread on the breadboard?   5. Is Jimmy throwing up in the bathroom?   6. Am I failing my science class?   7. Is Roger playing the bagpipes?   8. Are the children bursting the balloons?   9. Is the little boy showing me something?   10. Is the snail crawling on the tree?   11. Is Shane drawing a maple leaf?   12. Are the seals playing in the waves?   13. Are they swimming in the pool with their water wings?   14. Is Chris grating the cheese with the grater?   15. Are they kidding?   16. Is he shuffling the cards?   17. Is Grace sobbing in her bedroom?   18. Is the dog wagging its tail?

33 The Past Progressive (Continuous) Tense

33-1   1. The laboratory was testing the blood for AIDS and other diseases.   2. We were walking in the snow with our snowshoes.   3. The mechanic was lowering the car when it fell.   4. The girls were talking on the phone for two hours.   5. I was changing the lightbulb when I got a shock.   6. The kids were rolling down the mountain.   7. She was placing a wig on her head when I entered.   8. George was listening to music with his headphones.   9. Vance was covering his answers during the test.   10. We were buying a gift for the christening.   11. I was dropping a quarter in the tollbooth when he rammed the back of my car.   12. My daughter was blowing her nose.   13. The lights were glowing in the distance.   14. They were struggling to keep the files up-to-date.   15. We were dividing our time between the Grand Canyon and the casinos.

33-2   1. were blooming   2. was eating   3. was crushing   4. was warning   5. was welcoming   6. was putting   7. were wearing   8. were playing   9. were hiding   10. was reading   11. was wearing   12. was talking   13. were crying   14. was grieving   15. were weaving   16. was combing   17. was scolding   18. was working   19. were frightening   20. was gambling   21. were flying   22. was acting   23. were reaching   24. was sweeping   25. were hatching   26. was putting

34 The Past Progressive (Continuous) Tense: Negative Form

34-1   1. She was not getting chemotherapy treatments for lung cancer. She wasn't getting chemotherapy treatments for lung cancer.   2. My stomach was not growling in class this morning. My stomach wasn't growling in class this morning.   3. We were not driving on the wrong side of the road. We weren't driving on the wrong side of the road.   4. He was not smiling at you. He wasn't smiling at you.   5. It was not nipping my ankle. It wasn't nipping my ankle.   6. The collar was not choking the dog. The collar wasn't choking the dog.   7. Tania was not succeeding in her course and she quit. Tania wasn't succeeding in her course and she quit.   8. The guests were not eating the potato salad. The guests weren't eating the potato salad.   9. They were not joking. They weren't joking.

34-2   1. wasn't snipping   2. wasn't working   3. weren't overdoing   4. wasn't relying   5. wasn't carrying   6. weren't making   7. wasn't carving   8. wasn't coping   9. wasn't slurring   10. weren't diving   11. wasn't tasting   12. weren't feeding   13. wasn't cleaning   14. wasn't flapping   15. weren't distracting   16. wasn't dripping   17. wasn't wearing   18. weren't sitting   19. weren't jumping   20. weren't rotting   21. wasn't hovering   22. wasn't petting   23. weren't counting   24. wasn't wearing   25. wasn't breathing   26. weren't laughing

35 The Past Progressive (Continuous) Tense: Question Form

35-1   1. Were the police stopping everyone at the corner?   2. Was my yellow rubber duck floating in the bath?   3. Was the meat thawing on the counter?   4. Were the wounds on his body healing?   5. Was she hoping for a new nightgown for Christmas?   6. Was the ice cracking on the lake?   7. Was the beautiful peacock attracting a lot of attention?   8. Was she buying watermelon and corn on the cob for the picnic?   9. Were the actors rehearsing for the play?   10. Was it drifting on the sea?   11. Were they using matches to light the candles on the cake?   12. Were you swimming with goggles and a snorkel?   13. Was Réal grabbing the bull by the horns?   14. Was she taking vitamins during her pregnancy?   15. Was the housekeeper dusting the furniture?

35-2   1. Was she starting her car?   2. Were they begging us to stay for supper?   3. Were we closing the store early?   4. Were they walking barefoot on the pebbles?   5. Was the dog panting?   6. Were you scratching your elbow?   7. Was she measuring her waist and hips?   8. Was Danny daring me to jump in the lake?   9. Was it eating my peanut butter sandwich?   10. Were you ripping my sweater?   11. Was Gary omitting the details?   12. Was it following me?   13. Were the detectives investigating the crime?   14. Was he spitting on the sidewalk?   15. Were they raising goats?   16. Were you pretending to be a big ape?   17. Was I reading the right letter?   18. Was the ox pulling the cart?

36 Prepositions: *From* and *Of*

36-1   1. We gave her a beautiful bouquet of flowers.   2. I got a toothbrush from my dentist.   3. He is a member of the hockey hall of fame.   4. She sent me a postcard from Canada.   5. Peter is a man of many talents.   6. We heard voices from beyond the bushes.   7. He called me from a pay phone.   8. I need a cup of sugar for this recipe.   9. Is that guy from Mexico?   10. I work from Monday to Thursday. I don't work Friday.   11. Do you want a glass of beer?   12. She is a woman of value in our company.   13. The cat jumped from the couch to the window.   14. Open the gift from me.

36-2   1. of   2. of   3. from   4. of   5. from   6. of   7. of   8. from   9. of   10. of, from   11. of   12. of   13. from   14. of   15. from   16. from   17. of   18. of   19. of   20. from   21. of   22. from   23. from   24. from   25. of   26. from   27. of   28. from   29. from   30. of   31. of   32. from   33. of   34. from   35. of   36. from   37. of   38. from

37 *Will*: Future Tense

37-1   1. I will climb to the top of the lighthouse to see the ships.   2. You will become a rich and famous author.   3. The government will reduce taxes next year.   4. The fairy will grant you several wishes.   5. My mother will make a cherry pie.   6. We will study the brain in my science class.   7. They will enlarge the picture of the swordfish that they caught.   8. We will gather blueberries, strawberries, and raspberries to make jam.   9. He will hug and kiss you when he sees you.   10. Brad will introduce me to his parents tomorrow night.   11. We will ship the package to you this afternoon.   12. Mary will envy your friendship with Paul.   13. The government will ban tobacco in all public places.   14. She will pamper her new baby.   15. I will flip the pancakes now.

37-2   1. will calculate   2. will balance   3. will develop   4. will concentrate   5. will last   6. will postpone   7. will learn   8. will tame   9. will tell   10. will wonder   11. will order   12. will move   13. will miss   14. will bake   15. will continue   16. will be   17. will nod   18. will use   19. will get   20. will stimulate   21. will cause   22. will donate   23. will inform   24. will share

38 *Will*: Future Tense: Negative Form

38-1   1. He will not declare bankruptcy. He won't declare bankruptcy.   2. My neighbor will not trim his bushes. My neighbor won't trim his bushes.   3. John will not trim his sideburns. John won't trim his sideburns.   4. Anna will not go on a blind date. Anna won't go on a blind date.   5. You will not recognize me with my wig. You won't recognize me with my wig.   6. They will not allow you to stay overnight. They won't allow you to stay overnight.   7. We will not celebrate on New Year's Eve. We won't celebrate on New Year's Eve.   8. The man will not confess to the murder. The man won't confess to the murder.   9. I will not pawn my guitar. I won't pawn my guitar.

38-2   1. won't ruin   2. won't clog   3. won't issue   4. won't improve   5. won't guess   6. won't discuss   7. won't benefit   8. won't delay   9. won't compensate   10. won't allow   11. won't cure   12. won't

purchase   13. won't listen   14. won't attempt   15. won't wear   16. won't sign   17. won't make
18. won't operate   19. won't betray   20. won't remove   21. won't have   22. won't live   23. won't
mean   24. won't tolerate   25. won't hand   26. won't fail

39   *Will*: Future Tense: Question Form

39-1   1. Will the snow disappear in the spring?   2. Will your mother punish you for that?   3. Will the police accuse Sara?   4. Will you spell your last name for me?   5. Will she throw her old pajamas in the garbage?   6. Will he measure it with his brand-new tape measure?   7. Will Bobby show the judges his muscles?   8. Will it poison you with its fangs?   9. Will they mention it to their foreman?   10. Will the gardener spray the wasps and bees with poison?   11. Will they rescue the eagles on the island?   12. Will your boyfriend partake in the writing competition?   13. Will we travel a lot next year?   14. Will it kick me?   15. Will she buy a new ironing board and toaster for her apartment?

39-2   1. Will it arrive on time?   2. Will he publish his report?   3. Will they blame me?   4. Will we be in rush hour traffic?   5. Will our country ban the sale of ivory?   6. Will Sheila stick the magnet on the fridge?   7. Will you close your mouth when you eat?   8. Will we produce a lot of corn this year?   9. Will our company expand next year?   10. Will it rain tomorrow?   11. Will we trade our trailer for a boat?   12. Will he pause the movie for a few minutes?   13. Will I regret it?   14. Will it grind the coffee beans?   15. Will you require stitches in your knee?   16. Will the roof sag with all the snow on it?   17. Will they bid on the famous painting?   18. Will I gain weight if I eat this?   19. Will he respond?   20. Will I have enough time?

40   *Be Going To*: Future Tense

40-1   1. I am going to hurry because I don't want to miss my bus.   2. He drank too much, and now he is going to vomit.   3. You are going to dirty my floor with your muddy shoes.   4. The sun is going to shine all day today.   5. I am going to wait for you in the lobby downstairs.   6. We are going to sell our waterbed in our garage sale.   7. The kids are going to swim in the shallow end of the pool.   8. The adults are going to dive in the deep end of the pool.   9. You are going to injure your back if you lift that heavy box.   10. It is going to create problems in the office.   11. I am going to spread the jam on my toast.   12. My manager is going to check his schedule for next week.   13. You are going to be upset if the audience doesn't applaud.   14. He is going to surprise her with a diamond ring.   15. She is going to remove your name from the list.

40-2   1. are, assume   2. is, suggest   3. is, tighten   4. am, clip   5. are, observe   6. am, give   7. is, seem   8. are, remind   9. are, admit   10. is, be   11. is, ask   12. am, tap   13. are, commute   14. are, skip   15. am, put   16. is, marry   17. is, occur   18. are, charge   19. is, belong   20. is, vanish   21. am, buy   22. are, be

41   *Be Going To*: Future Tense: Negative Form

41-1   1. My company is not going to announce cutbacks for the new year. My company isn't going to announce cutbacks for the new year.   2. We are not going to submit the report in the morning. We aren't going to submit the report in the morning.   3. I am not going to withdraw all my money. No contraction.   4. They are not going to invest the funds in the stock market. They aren't going to invest the funds in the stock market.   5. This experience is not going to haunt me for the rest of my life. This experience isn't going to haunt me for the rest of my life.   6. Annie is not going to chill the wine before she serves it. Annie isn't going to chill the wine before she serves it.   7. The ostrich is not going to attack you. The ostrich isn't going to attack you.   8. You are not going to reuse the bags. You aren't going to reuse the bags.   9. He is not going to divorce his wife. He isn't going to divorce his wife.

41-2   1. aren't   2. isn't   3. aren't   4. aren't   5. aren't   6. isn't   7. am not   8. aren't   9. isn't   10. aren't   11. isn't   12. am not   13. isn't   14. aren't   15. aren't   16. am not   17. isn't   18. aren't   19. isn't   20. isn't   21. aren't   22. isn't   23. isn't   24. aren't   25. aren't   26. isn't   27. isn't   28. aren't

42   *Be Going To*: Future Tense: Question Form

42-1   1. Is he going to share this knowledge with the world?   2. Is she going to cooperate with us?   3. Are you going to provide me with a good explanation?   4. Are they going to immigrate to the United States in

August?   5. Is it going to turn green when I put it in water?   6. Is the immigration office going to process my file in July?   7. Are my parents going to supply me with my school supplies in September?   8. Am I going to drain the vegetables with this?   9. Are they going to complete the project in November or December?   10. Is she going to apply for a new job in October?   11. Are you going to scrub the bathtub now?   12. Are the cows and horses going to graze in the field?   13. Are you going to dip the apple in honey?   14. Are we going to store the snowblower in the garage during the summer?   15. Is the teacher going to talk about war and peace in history class today?

42-2   1. Is he going to promise to be good?   2. Are you going to wish for a car again?   3. Am I going to compete with you?   4. Is she going to rest on the couch?   5. Are you going to fake that you are sick?   6. Is he going to break the icicles with the shovel?   7. Is Sonia going to buy new oven mitts?   8. Is the insurance company going to assess the damage?   9. Are you going to cry?   10. Is it going to be sunny tomorrow?   11. Am I going to have a second interview?   12. Are we going to wait a long time at customs?   13. Is she going to sort the dirty laundry?   14. Is Bobby going to tidy his room?   15. Are we going to watch the scary movie about the werewolf?   16. Are they going to whistle the song?   17. Are they going to bring shrimp to the party tomorrow night?   18. Is it going to be good?

43   The Indefinite Articles: A and *An*

43-1   1. We saw a horrible accident this morning.   2. This is a one-way street.   3. My uncle has an ostrich on his farm.   4. He is an American citizen.   5. I wear a uniform to work.   6. There was an earthquake last night.   7. You are an excellent student.   8. I need a hammer to fix the roof.   9. It was a useful tool. 10. I have a red apple in my lunch bag.   11. We bought an oil painting at the market.   12. This is a busy airport.   13. Give me an example, please.   14. We played the game for an hour and a half.

43-2   1. an, a, a   2. a   3. an, a   4. an   5. a, an, a   6. an   7. an   8. a   9. a   10. an   11. a   12. an, a, an   13. a   14. an, a, an, a, an   15. a, a   16. an   17. an   18. an   19. a, a   20. an, a   21. a   22. an   23. a   24. an   25. an, a   26. an   27. a   28. an   29. a   30. an   31. an   32. a, a, an   33. a   34. an, a, a   35. a, an   36. an   37. a   38. an   39. a   40. an

44   Irregular Verbs Table

No exercises

45   The Present Perfect Tense

45-1   1. They have worked in Japan.   2. William has grown a lot since the last time I saw him.   3. My parents have been together for twenty years.   4. They have borrowed a lot of money from their friends.   5. She has taught English in many different schools.   6. You have offended everybody in the office.   7. I have heard that noise in my car several times.   8. He has cheated on every one of his tests.   9. We have tried to help them.   10. It has taken a long time.

45-2   1. has broken   2. have used   3. have seen   4. has made   5. has bitten   6. have offered   7. have flown   8. have suffered   9. have torn   10. has forgiven   11. have known   12. has accused   13. has started   14. have discussed   15. have warned   16. has helped   17. have chosen   18. has sung   19. have thanked   20. has climbed

46   The Present Perfect Tense: Negative Form

46-1   1. My teacher has not written two books. My teacher hasn't written two books.   2. I have not accepted the offer. I haven't accepted the offer.   3. They have not invented many fun games. They haven't invented many fun games.   4. The light has not attracted all the bugs. The light hasn't attracted all the bugs.   5. Joe and Lynn have not become rich and famous. Joe and Lynn haven't become rich and famous.   6. We have not found that he works very hard. We haven't found that he works very hard.   7. Cassandra has not waited a long time for the news. Cassandra hasn't waited a long time for the news.

46-2   1. haven't kept   2. hasn't noticed   3. haven't gone   4. hasn't convinced   5. hasn't built   6. haven't done   7. hasn't expressed   8. haven't wasted   9. haven't given   10. haven't solved   11. hasn't had   12. haven't asked   13. hasn't beaten   14. haven't escaped   15. hasn't fallen   16. hasn't forgotten

47 The Present Perfect Tense: Question Form

47-1   1. Have you shown your report card to your parents?   2. Has the teacher corrected all the exams? 3. Have I brought enough for everybody?   4. Has my dog chewed all the furniture?   5. Has it followed me to school often?   6. Have we wrapped all the gifts?   7. Has she blown out all the candles on the cake? 8. Have they apologized many times?   9. Has he drawn many beautiful pictures for her?   10. Have we benefited from that?   11. Has it hidden the peanuts?   12. Have I paid all the bills?   13. Has the sun risen?   14. Have I awoken the baby again?

47-2   1. Have you ironed the clothes?   2. Has he driven many miles?   3. Has Leora answered all the questions? 4. Have they fed the animals?   5. Has it occurred a few times?   6. Have I read that book before?   7. Have we invested all our money?   8. Have I parked here before?   9. Have you lost a lot of weight?   10. Has he managed the company alone?   11. Has Elvis left the building?   12. Has it disappeared?   13. Has Robin met many famous people?   14. Has George slept late many times?

48 The Past Perfect Tense

48-1   1. We had decided to stay home when they asked us to go out for dinner.   2. They had sold their boat when they bought the motorcycle.   3. He had expected to see you before you left.   4. I had had supper, so I only ate the dessert.   5. My grandmother had died when I was born.   6. The rain had stopped, so we went for a walk.   7. I had done the laundry when he brought me his dirty clothes.   8. She had seen the movie before, so she went to bed.   9. The teacher had explained the lesson twice, but we didn't understand.   10. We had passed all our exams, so we celebrated all night.

48-2   1. had thrown   2. had sung   3. had opened   4. had ordered   5. had swept   6. had worried   7. had ridden   8. had run   9. had completed   10. had finished   11. had rung   12. had rescued   13. had cut 14. had divorced

49 The Past Perfect Tense: Negative Form

49-1   1. He had not held a baby before today. He hadn't held a baby before today.   2. It had not arrived, so I called the store. It hadn't arrived, so I called the store.   3. I had not noticed that you were standing there. I hadn't noticed that you were standing there.   4. She had not paid the phone bill, so I paid it. She hadn't paid the phone bill, so I paid it.   5. They had not seen that movie before, and they really enjoyed it. They hadn't seen that movie before, and they really enjoyed it.   6. We had not flown before, so we were very nervous on the airplane. We hadn't flown before, so we were very nervous on the airplane.   7. You had not followed the instructions, and you made a mistake. You hadn't followed the instructions, and you made a mistake.

49-2   1. hadn't eaten   2. hadn't cleaned   3. hadn't rained   4. hadn't driven   5. hadn't hung   6. hadn't talked   7. hadn't bought   8. hadn't sent   9. hadn't had   10. hadn't borrowed   11. hadn't given 12. hadn't waited   13. hadn't smoked   14. hadn't drunk   15. hadn't started   16. hadn't made

50 The Past Perfect Tense: Question Form

50-1   1. Had he known that you were my brother?   2. Had they withdrawn all the money from their savings account?   3. Had you tried to ski before you bought the skis?   4. Had the play ended when she arrived? 5. Had you given him your phone number?   6. Had your aunt worn this dress before?   7. Had they tasted seafood before today?   8. Had Richard and Jennifer planned their vacation together?   9. Had Wade made coffee for everybody?   10. Had you had your breakfast before you went to school?   11. Had the teacher spoken to you before she called your parents?   12. Had it happened before?   13. Had you seen that woman before she came to your house?   14. Had they lived in Ontario before they moved to British Columbia?

50-2   1. Had she realized what she did?   2. Had you taken the wrong bus?   3. Had it seemed fair to everyone? 4. Had your boss brought his dog to work before today?   5. Had Tony been in the hospital before he had his operation?   6. Had they left the building before the fire started?   7. Had Jessica worked as a flight attendant before she became a nurse?   8. Had he taken the time to do it right?   9. Had they noticed where you put it?   10. Had you paid cash for it?   11. Had Maria found a new job before she quit her old job? 12. Had he played hockey before he joined our team?   13. Had you read the contract before you signed it?   14. Had it belonged to your grandmother before your mother gave it to you?